KU-000-919

Grandville

A Fantasy

by Bryan Talbot

Bryan Talbot (signature)

JONATHAN CAPE · LONDON

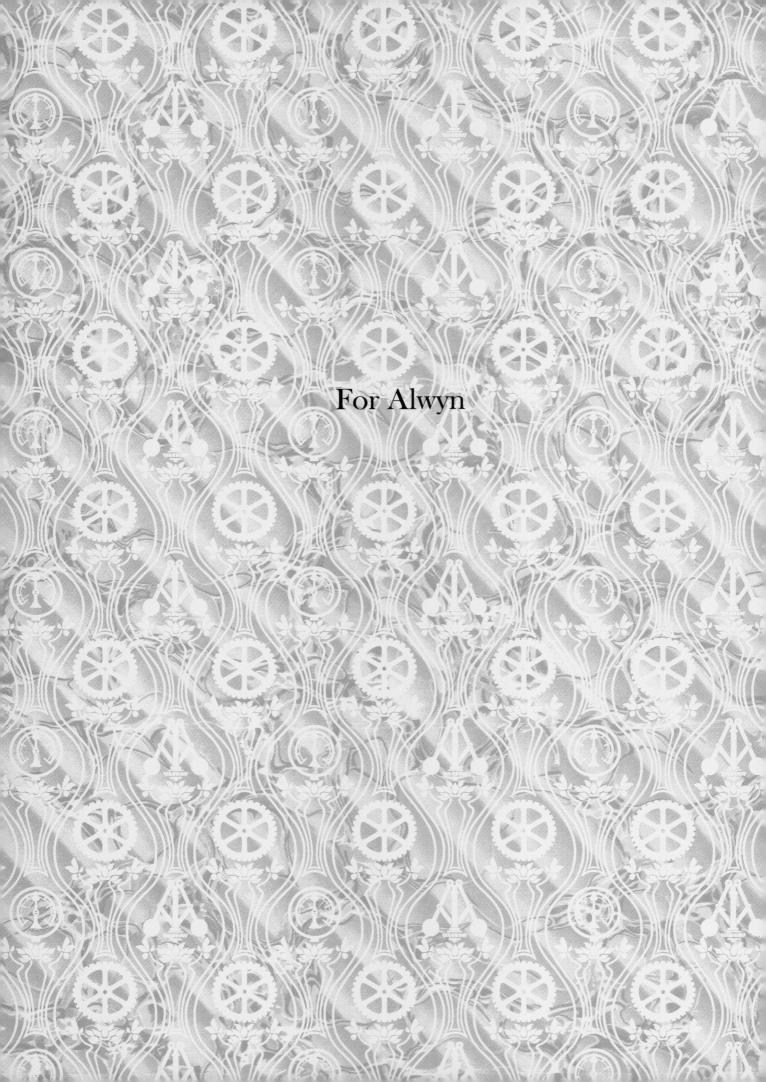

For Alwyn

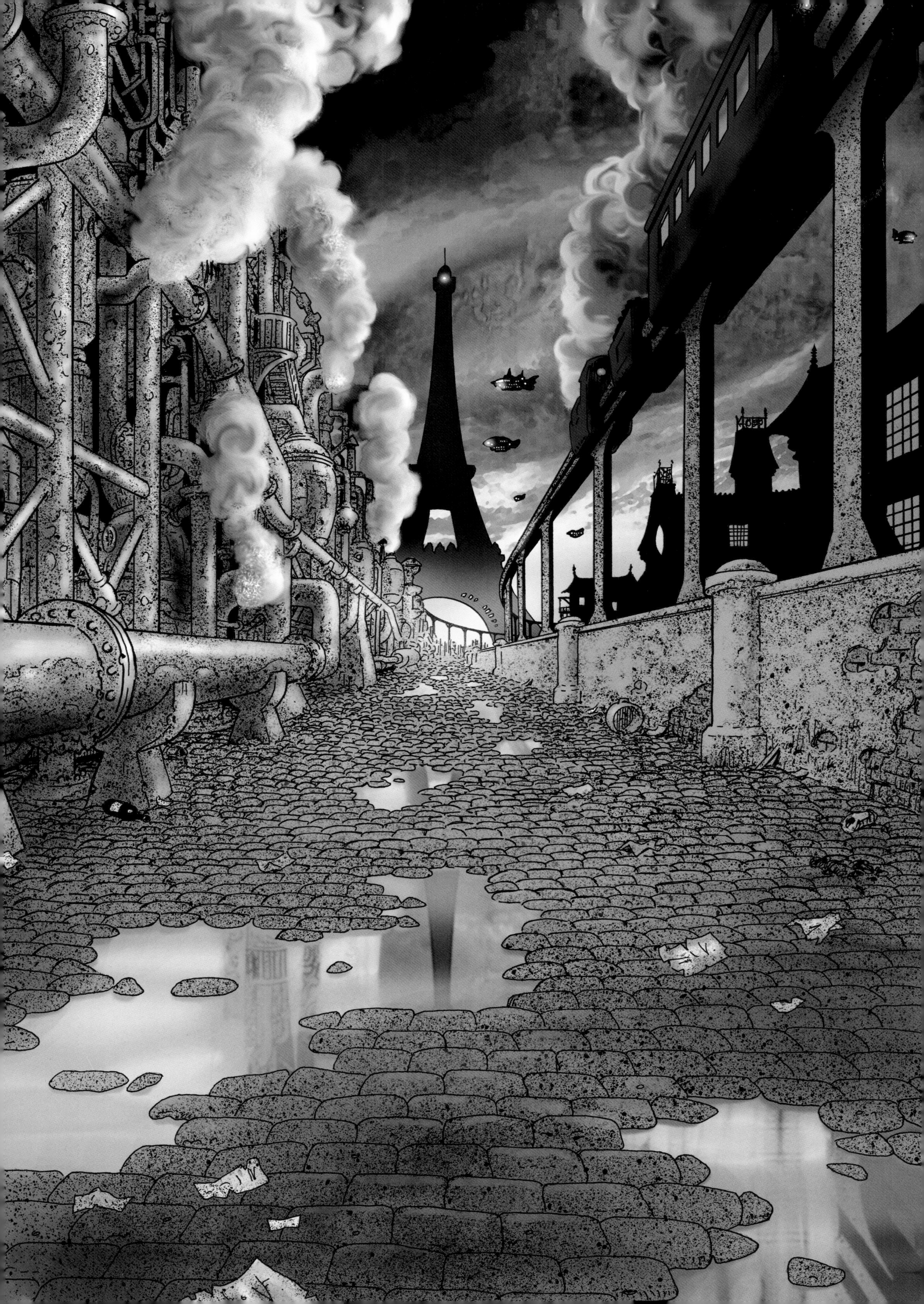

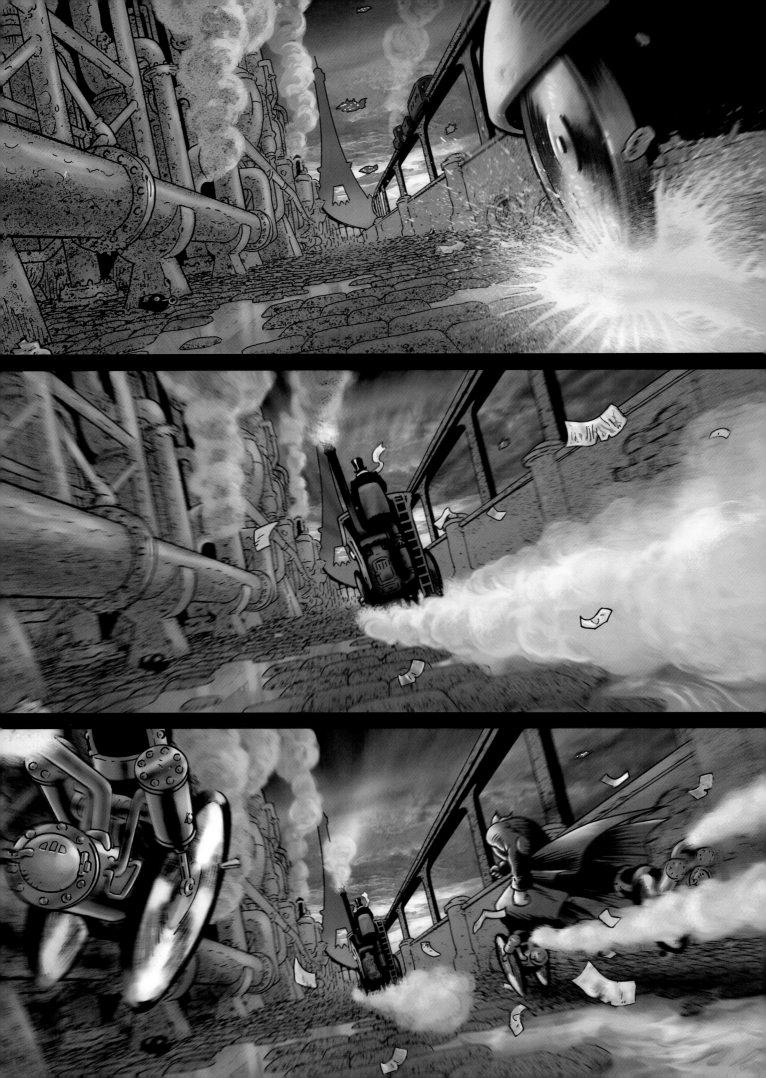

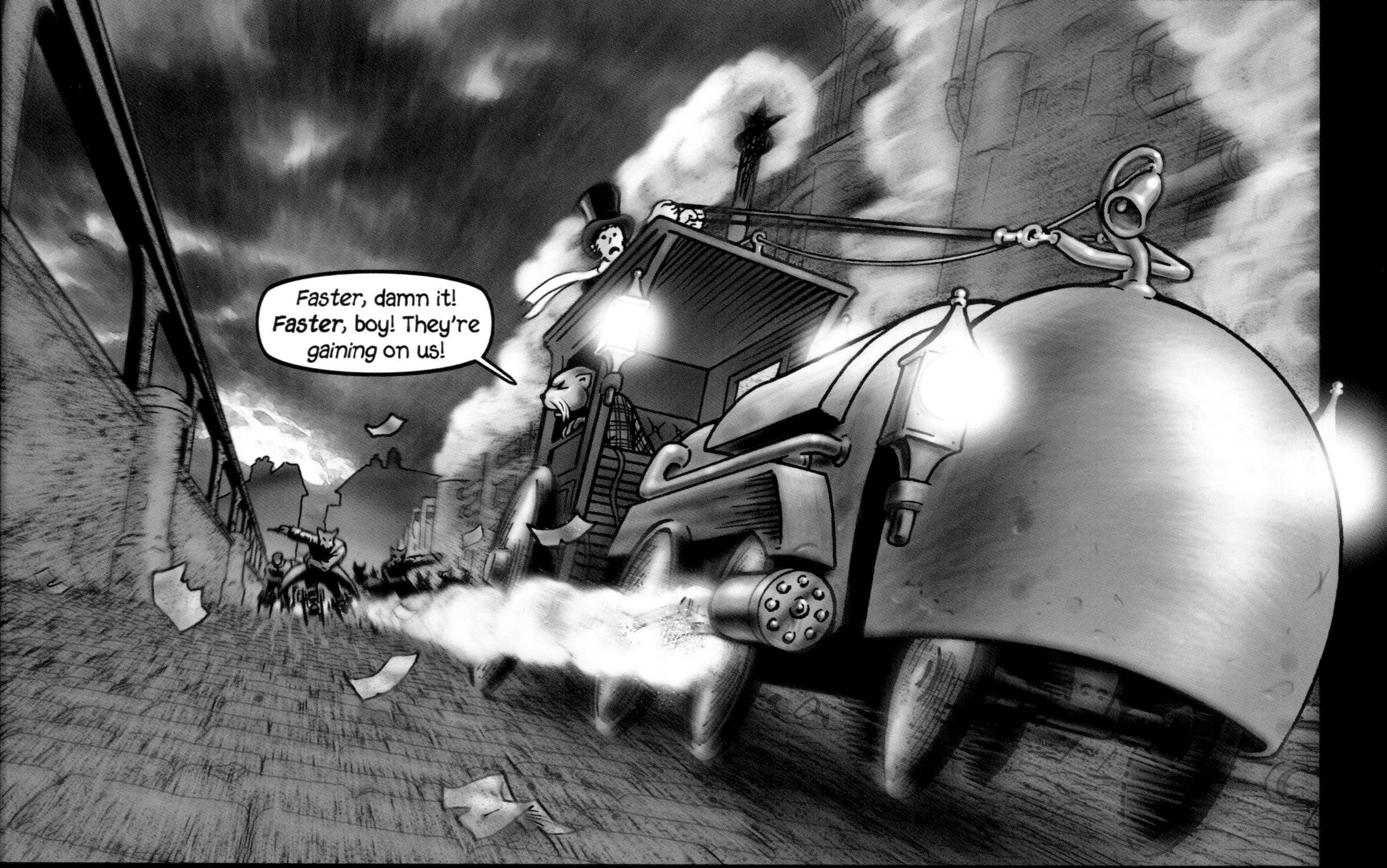
Faster, damn it! Faster, boy! They're gaining on us!
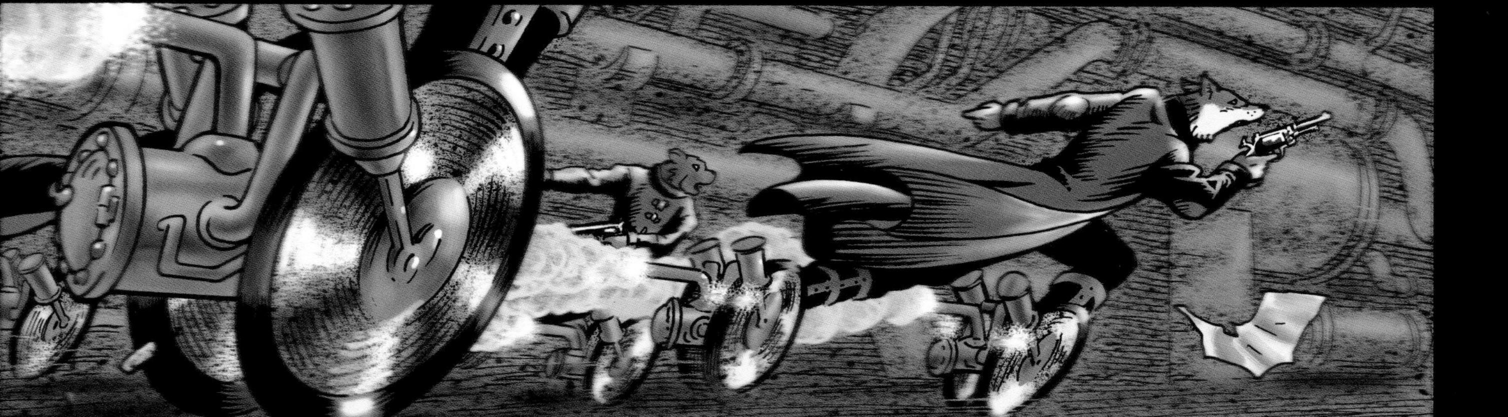
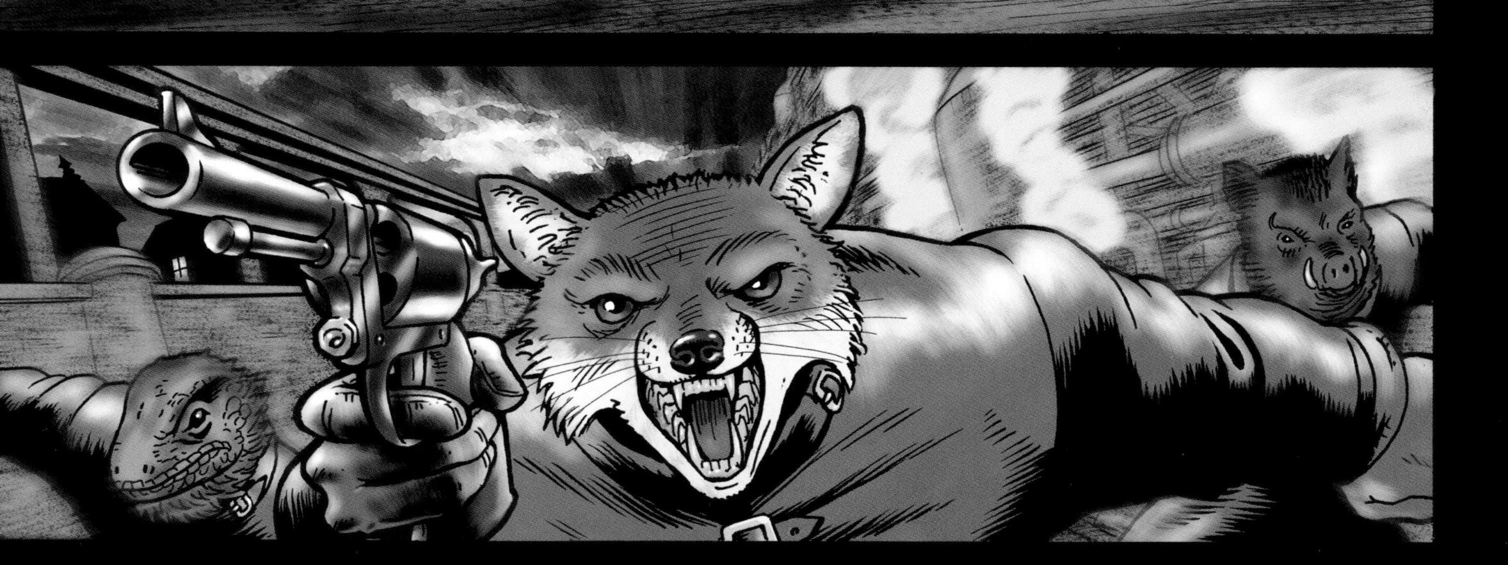

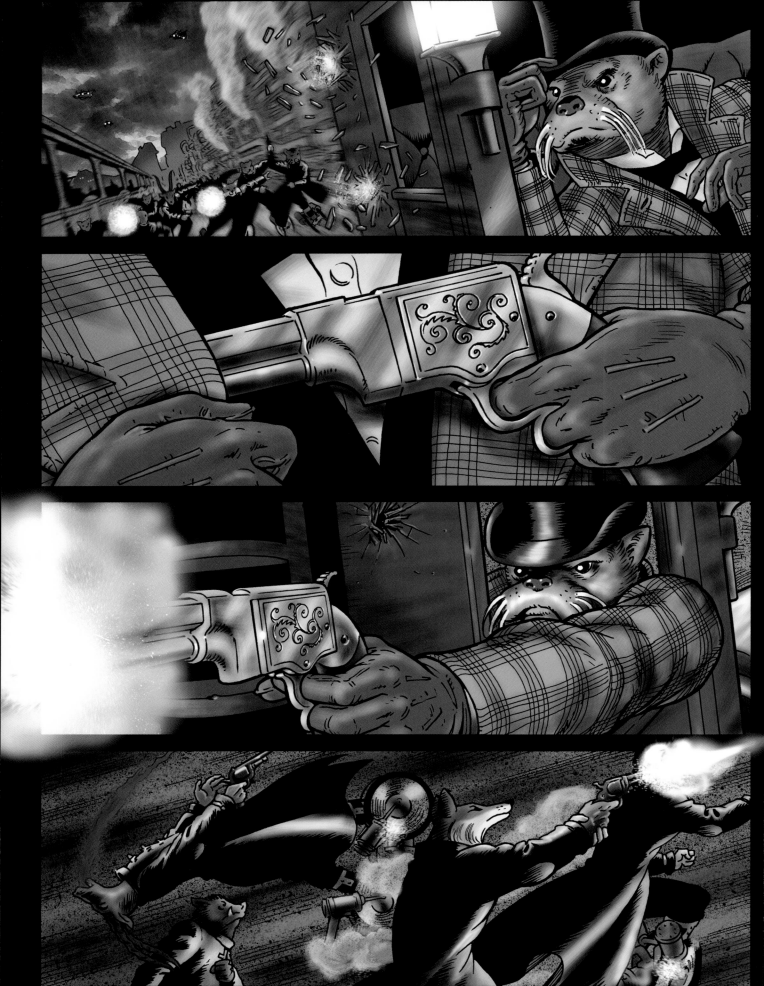

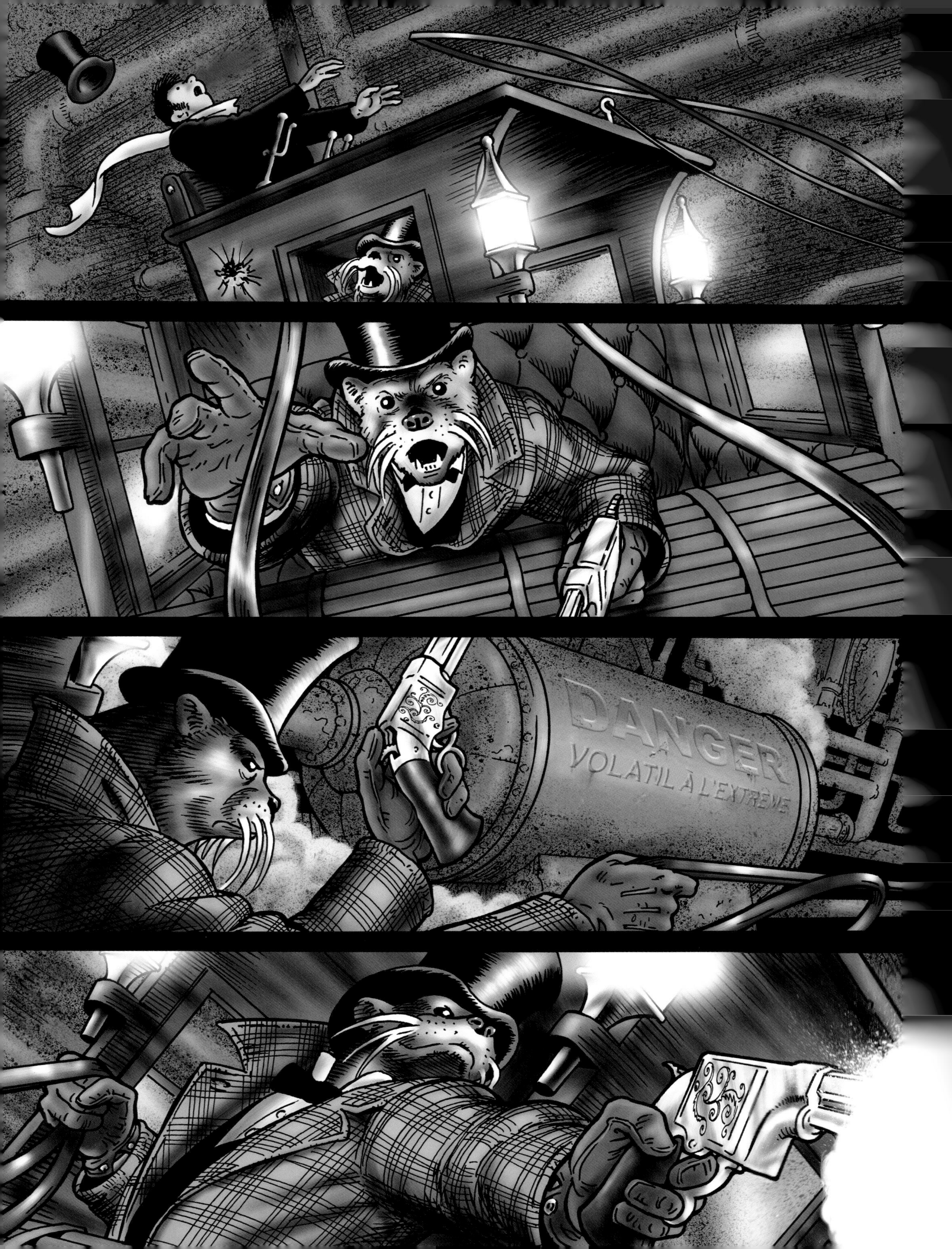
DANGER
VOLATIL À L'EXTRÊME

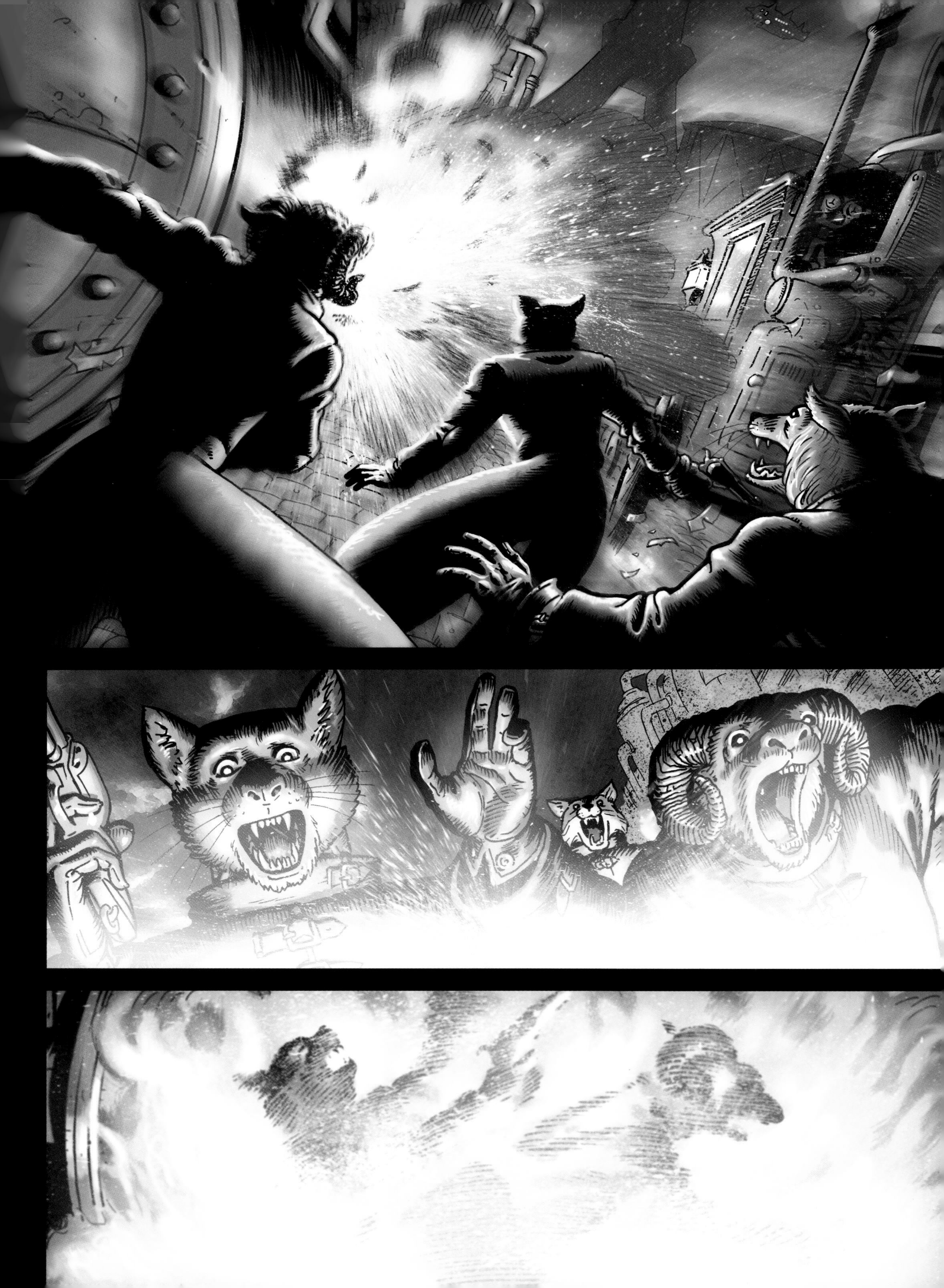

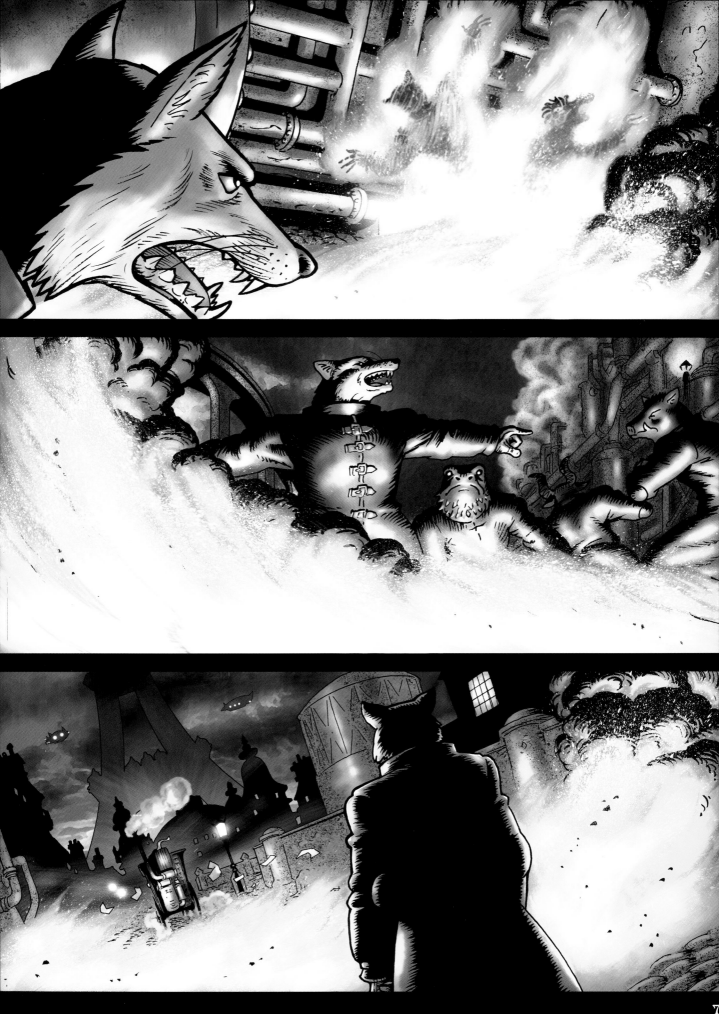

Grandville

A Fantasy

by
Bryan Talbot

Script, art & book design: Bryan Talbot

This story was inspired by the work of
the French caricaturist Jean Ignace Isidore Gérard (1803 –1847),
who worked under the nom-de-plume JJ Grandville,
and the seminal science fiction illustrator,
fellow Frenchman Albert Robida (1848 - 1926)

Not to mention Sir Arthur Conan Doyle, Rupert the Bear
and Quentin Tarantino

Bryan Talbot lettering font produced by Comicraft
Colour flats pages 26 – 98: Jordan Smith
French Advisor: Marie-Paul Brown

Art Nouveau steampunk pattern by Bryan Talbot,
based on the endpapers of "Dampf und Elektricität:
die Technik im Anfange des XX Jahrhunderts."
Berlin: W. Herlet. [c.1900]

Sincere acknowledgements for proof-reading,
comments on the work-in-progress and other important input to
Chaz Brenchley, Eric Bufkens, Dan Franklin, Nat Gertler, Dr Mel Gibson.
Paul Gravett, Jordan Smith, Dr Mary Talbot, Sylvie Toll and Chris Warner

No animals were harmed in the making of this book

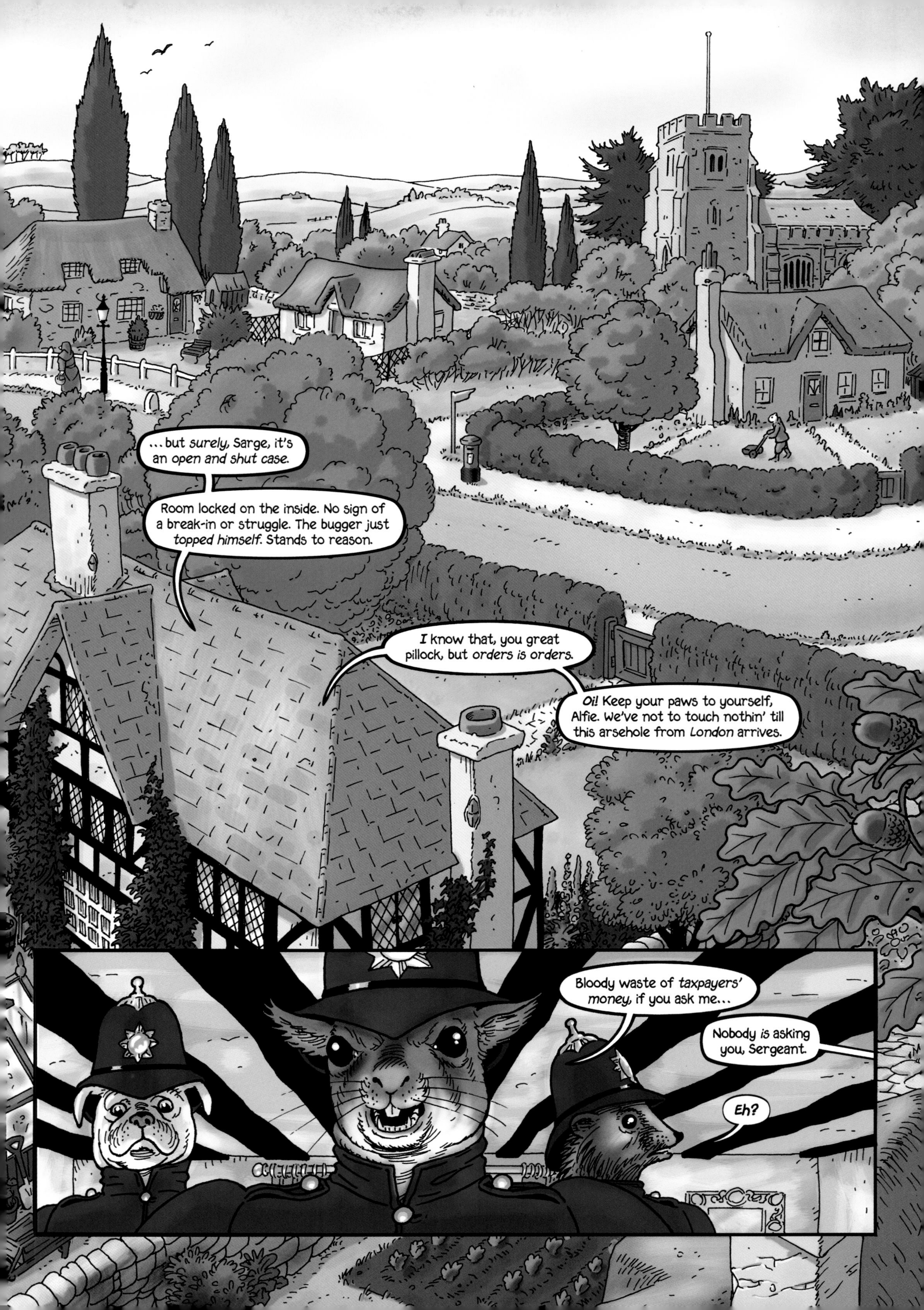

...but *surely*, Sarge, it's an *open and shut case*.
Room locked on the inside. No sign of a break-in or struggle. The bugger just *topped himself*. Stands to reason.
I know that, you great pillock, but *orders is orders*.
Oi! Keep your paws to yourself, Alfie. We've not to touch nothin' till this arsehole from *London* arrives.
Bloody waste of *taxpayers' money*, if you ask me...
Nobody *is* asking you, Sergeant.
Eh?

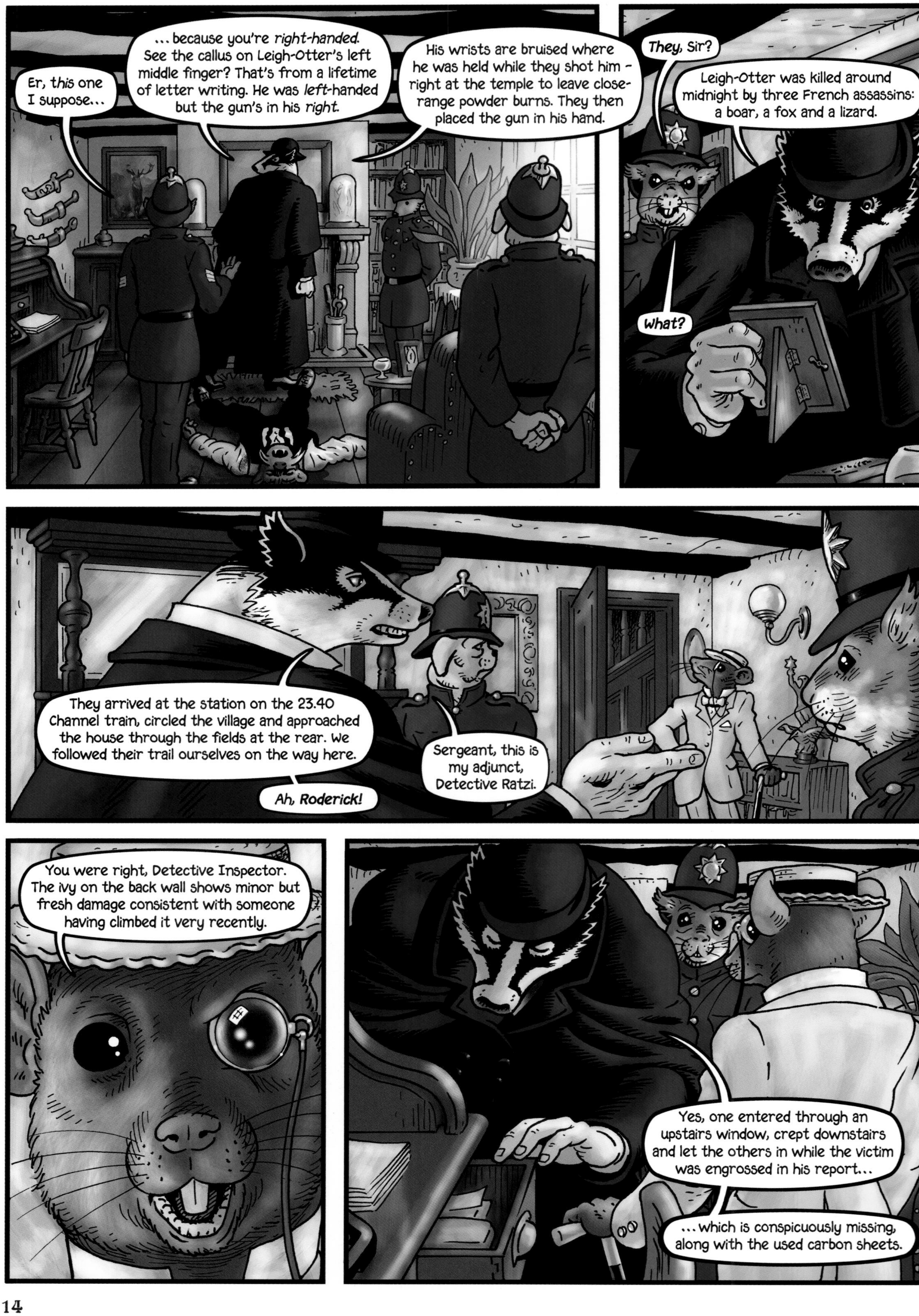
Er, this one I suppose...
...because you're right-handed. See the callus on Leigh-Otter's left middle finger? That's from a lifetime of letter writing. He was left-handed but the gun's in his right.
His wrists are bruised where he was held while they shot him - right at the temple to leave close-range powder burns. They then placed the gun in his hand.
They, Sir?
Leigh-Otter was killed around midnight by three French assassins: a boar, a fox and a lizard.
What?
They arrived at the station on the 23.40 Channel train, circled the village and approached the house through the fields at the rear. We followed their trail ourselves on the way here.
Ah, Roderick!
Sergeant, this is my adjunct, Detective Ratzi.
You were right, Detective Inspector. The ivy on the back wall shows minor but fresh damage consistent with someone having climbed it very recently.
Yes, one entered through an upstairs window, crept downstairs and let the others in while the victim was engrossed in his report...
...which is conspicuously missing, along with the used carbon sheets.

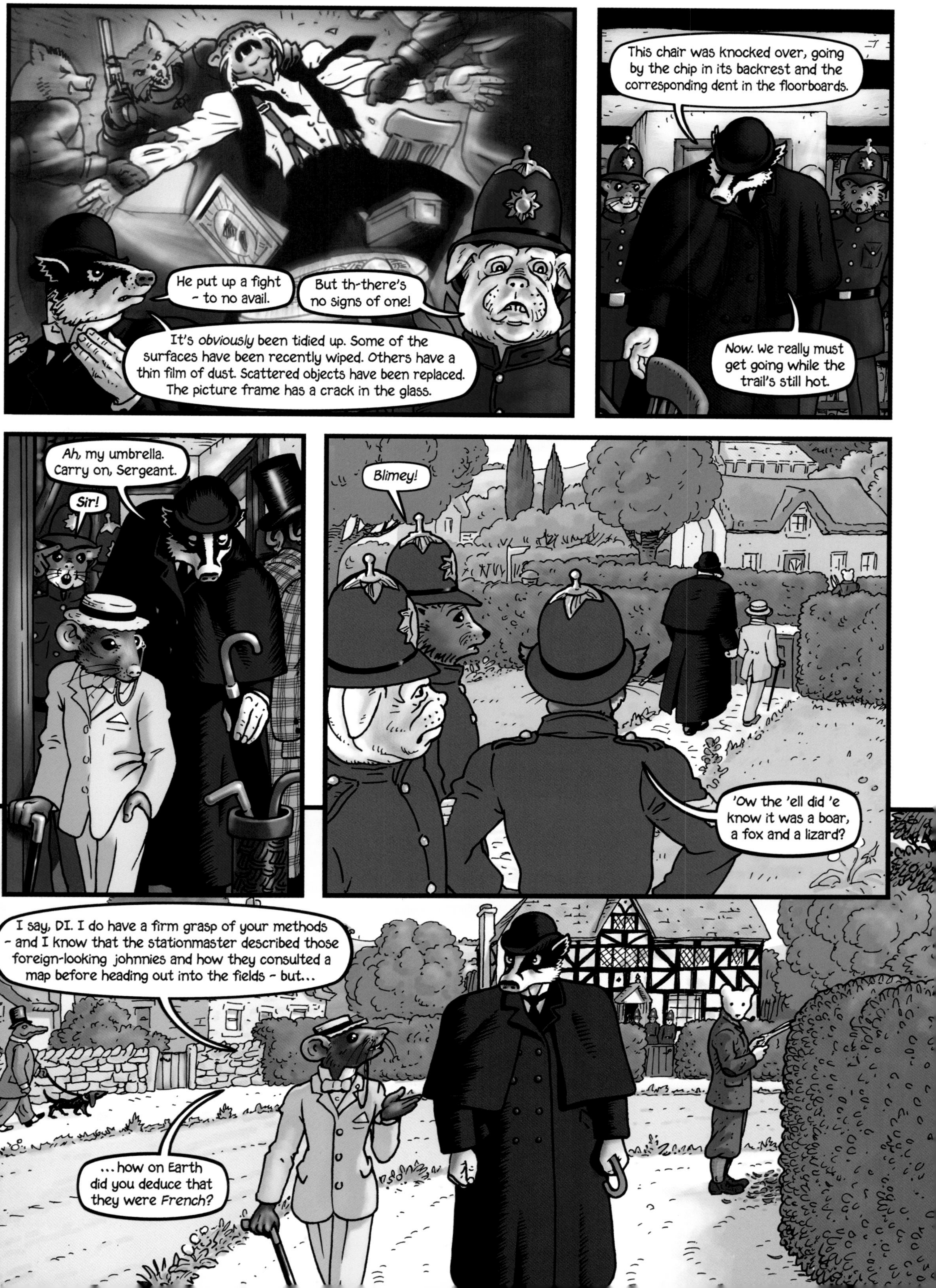
He put up a fight - to no avail.
But th-there's no signs of one!
It's *obviously* been tidied up. Some of the surfaces have been recently wiped. Others have a thin film of dust. Scattered objects have been replaced. The picture frame has a crack in the glass.
This chair was knocked over, going by the chip in its backrest and the corresponding dent in the floorboards.
Now. We really must get going while the trail's still hot.
Ah, my umbrella. Carry on, Sergeant.
Sir!
Blimey!
'Ow the 'ell did 'e know it was a boar, a fox and a lizard?
I say, DI. I do have a firm grasp of your methods - and I know that the stationmaster described those foreign-looking johnnies and how they consulted a map before heading out into the fields - but...
...how on Earth did you deduce that they were *French*?

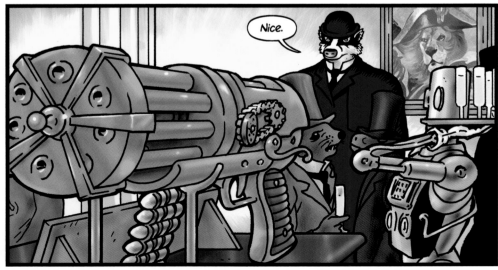

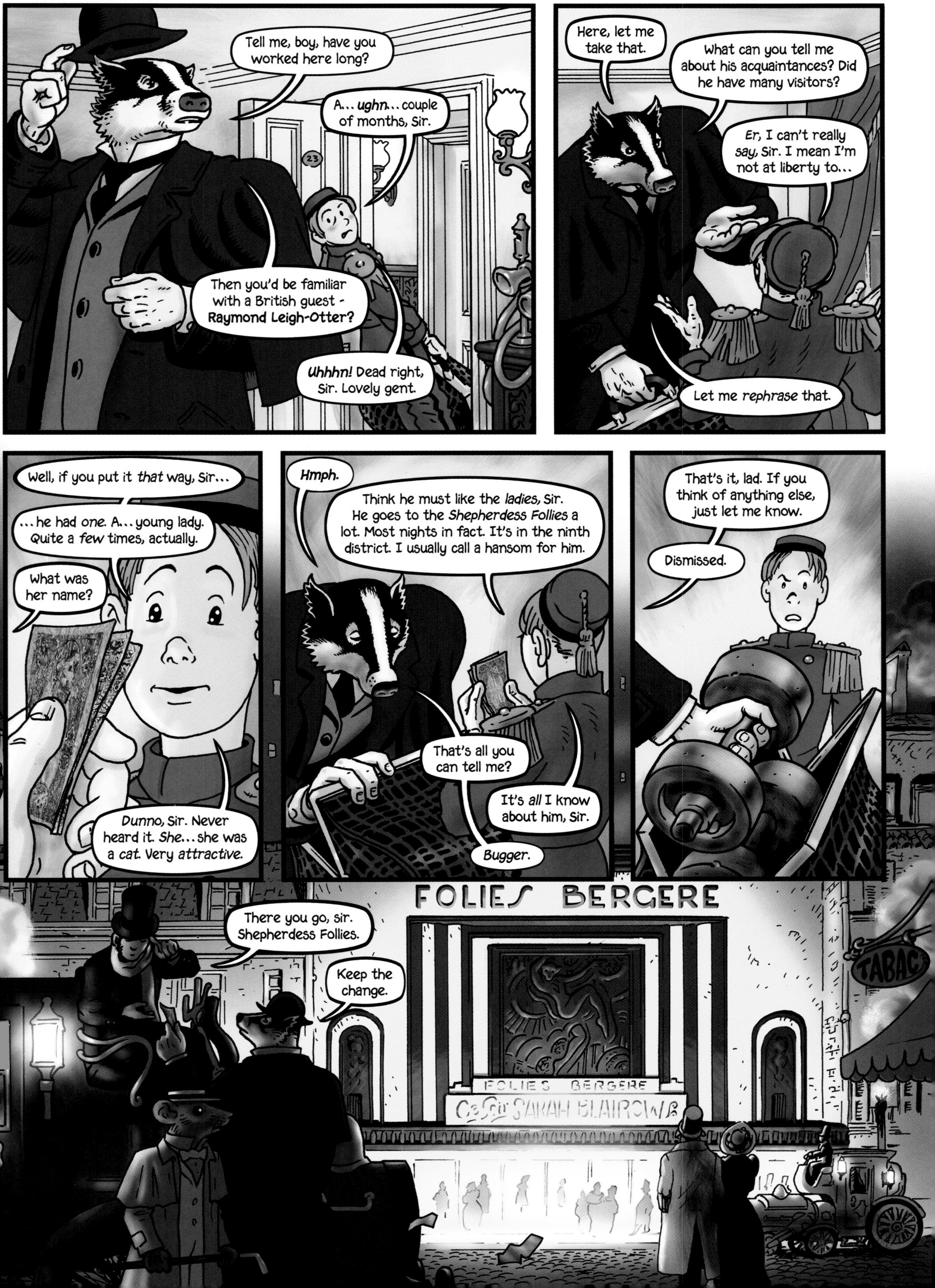
Tell me, boy, have you worked here long?
A... ughn... couple of months, Sir.
Then you'd be familiar with a British guest - Raymond Leigh-Otter?
Uhhhn! Dead right, Sir. Lovely gent.
Here, let me take that.
What can you tell me about his acquaintances? Did he have many visitors?
Er, I can't really say, Sir. I mean I'm not at liberty to...
Let me rephrase that.
Well, if you put it that way, Sir...
...he had one. A... young lady. Quite a few times, actually.
What was her name?
Dunno, Sir. Never heard it. She... she was a cat. Very attractive.
Hmph.
Think he must like the ladies, Sir. He goes to the Shepherdess Follies a lot. Most nights in fact. It's in the ninth district. I usually call a hansom for him.
That's all you can tell me?
It's all I know about him, Sir.
Bugger.
That's it, lad. If you think of anything else, just let me know.
Dismissed.
FOLIES BERGERE
There you go, sir. Shepherdess Follies.
Keep the change.
TABAC
FOLIES BERGERE

Anarchist scum! Long live Napoleon!

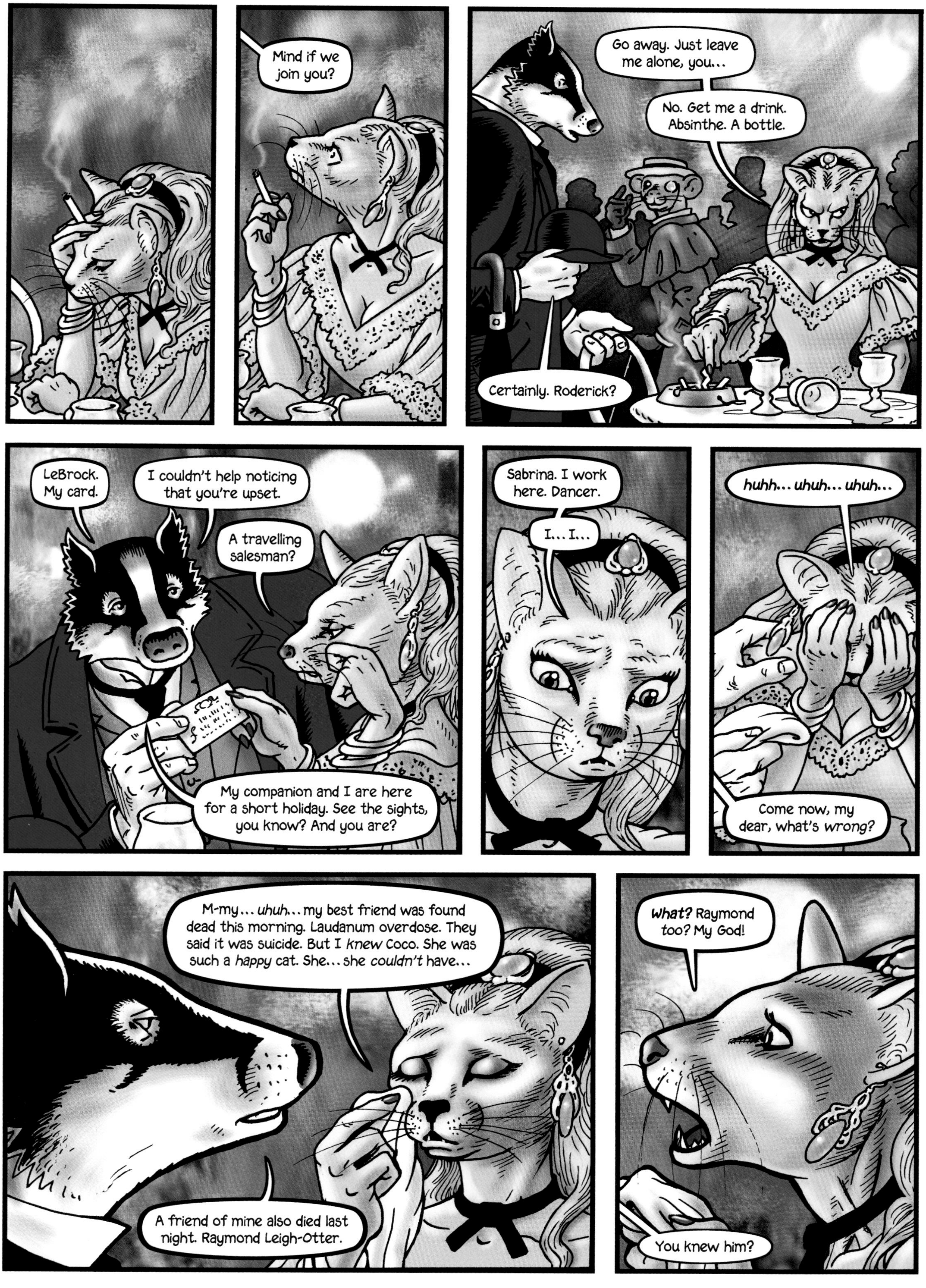
Mind if we join you?
Go away. Just leave me alone, you...
No. Get me a drink. Absinthe. A bottle.
Certainly. Roderick?
LeBrock. My card.
I couldn't help noticing that you're upset.
A travelling salesman?
My companion and I are here for a short holiday. See the sights, you know? And you are?
Sabrina. I work here. Dancer.
I... I...
huhh... uhuh... uhuh...
Come now, my dear, what's *wrong*?
M-my... *uhuh*... my best friend was found dead this morning. Laudanum overdose. They said it was suicide. But I *knew* Coco. She was such a *happy* cat. She... she *couldn't* have...
A friend of mine also died last night. Raymond Leigh-Otter.
What? Raymond too? My God!
You knew him?

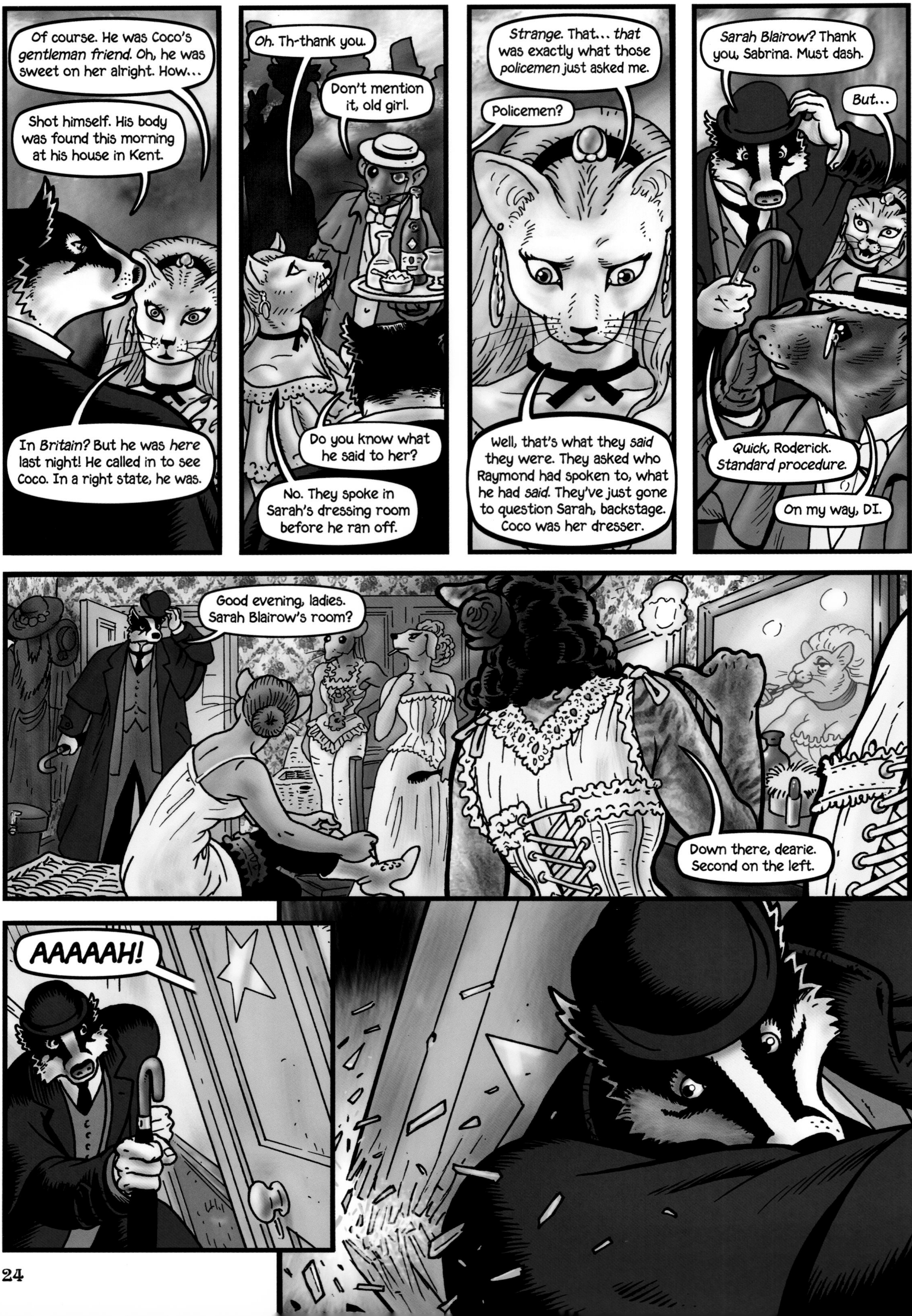
Of course. He was Coco's *gentleman friend.* Oh, he was sweet on her alright. How...
Shot himself. His body was found this morning at his house in Kent.
In *Britain?* But he was *here* last night! He called in to see Coco. In a right state, he was.
Oh. Th-thank you.
Don't mention it, old girl.
Do you know what he said to her?
No. They spoke in Sarah's dressing room before he ran off.
Strange. That... *that* was exactly what those *policemen* just asked me.
Policemen?
Well, that's what they *said* they were. They asked who Raymond had spoken to, what he had *said.* They've just gone to question Sarah, backstage. Coco was her dresser.
Sarah Blairow? Thank you, Sabrina. Must dash.
But...
Quick, Roderick. *Standard procedure.*
On my way, DI.
Good evening, ladies. Sarah Blairow's room?
Down there, dearie. Second on the left.
AAAAAH!

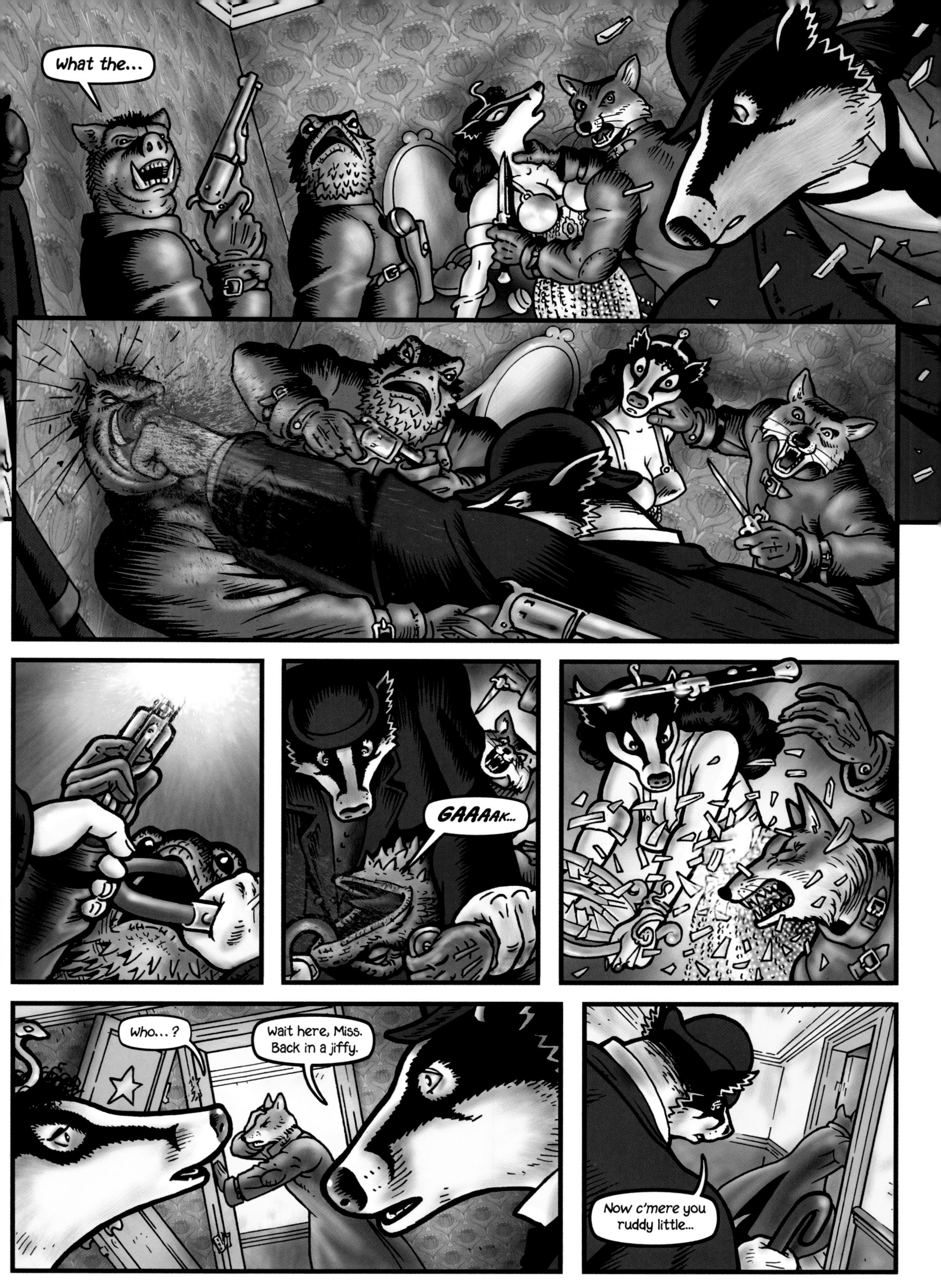
What the...
GAAAAK...
Who...?
Wait here, Miss.
Back in a jiffy.
Now c'mere you ruddy little...

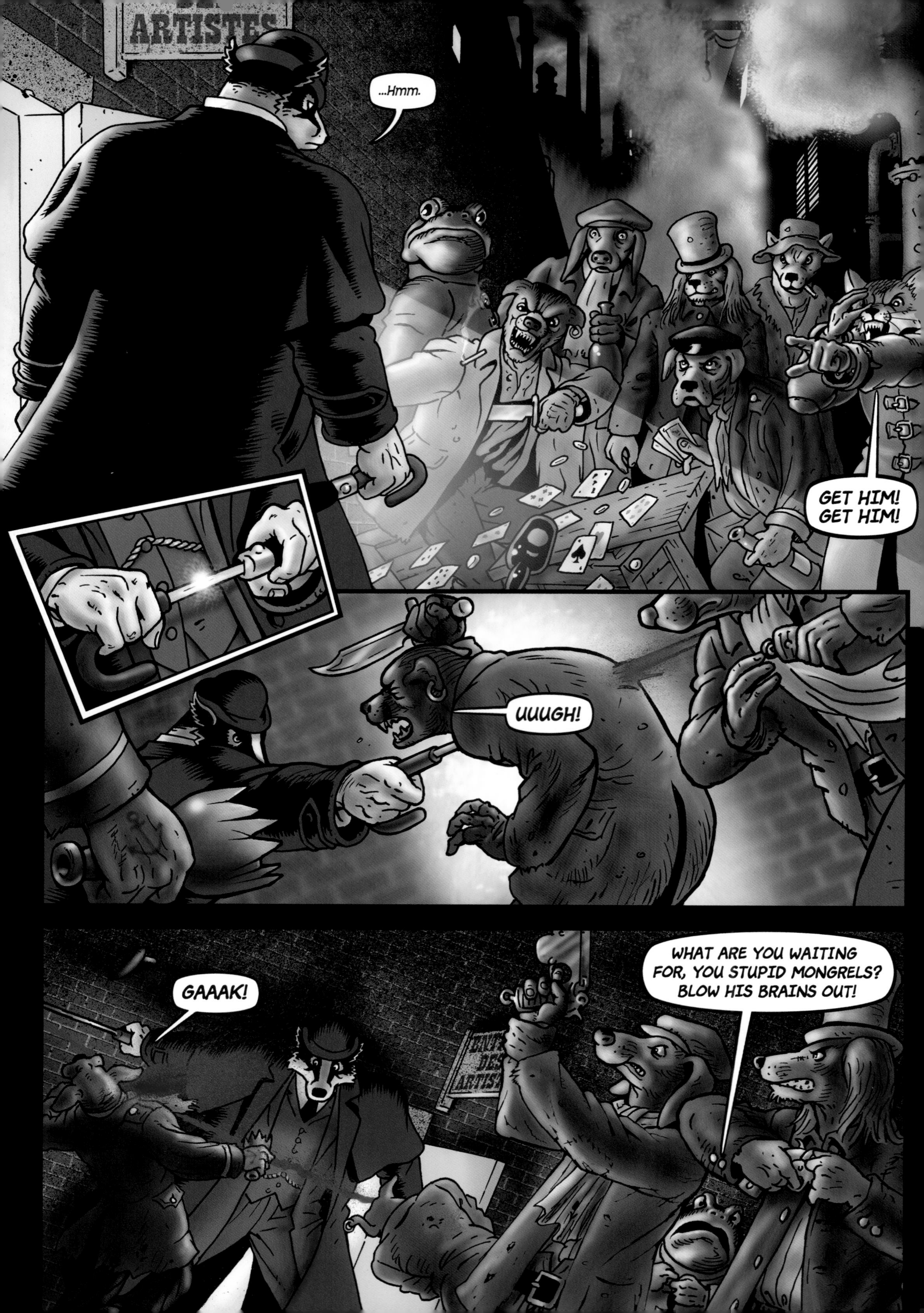
ARTISTES
...Hmm.
GET HIM! GET HIM!
UUUGH!
GAAAK!
WHAT ARE YOU WAITING FOR, YOU STUPID MONGRELS? BLOW HIS BRAINS OUT!

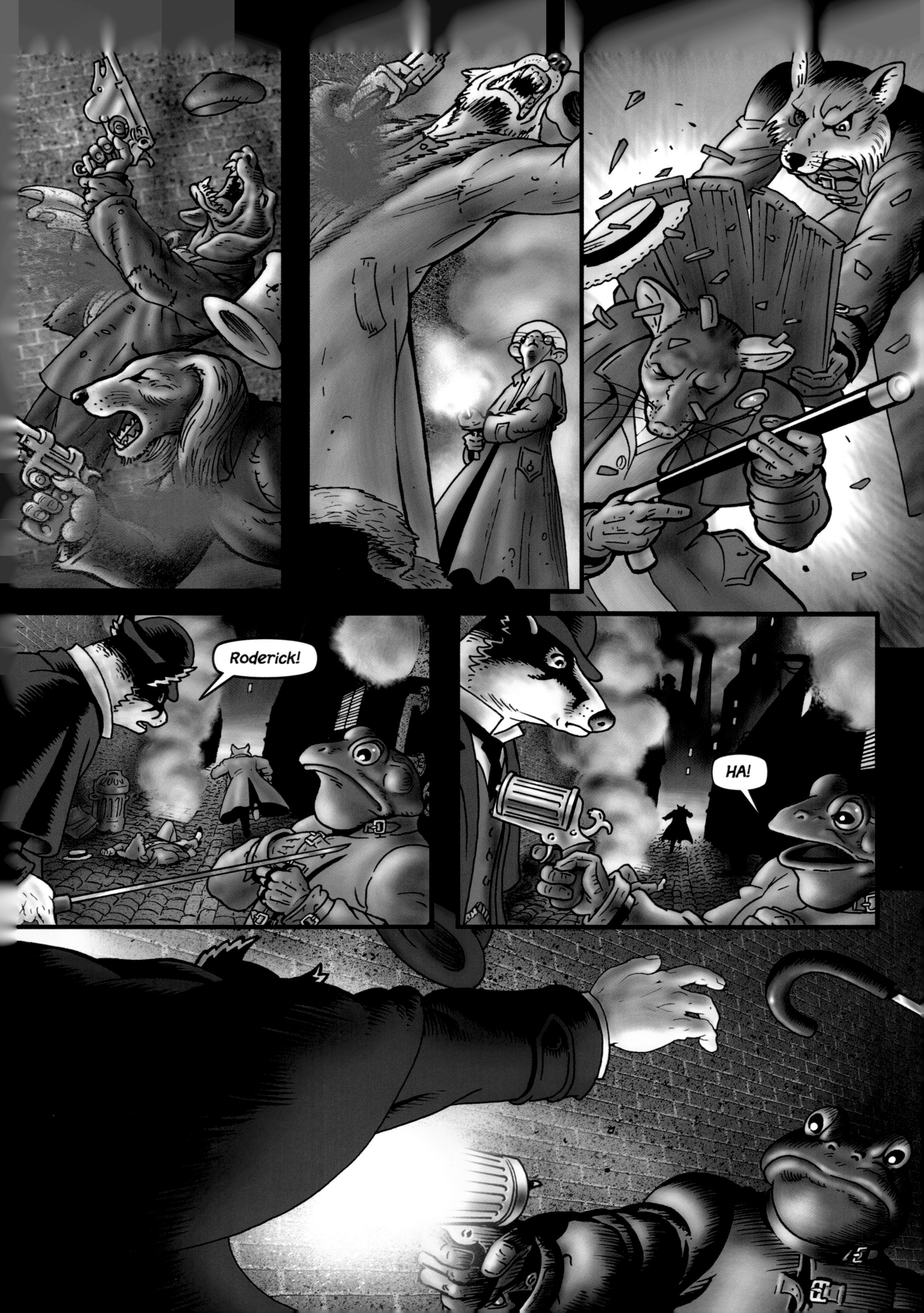
Roderick!
HA!

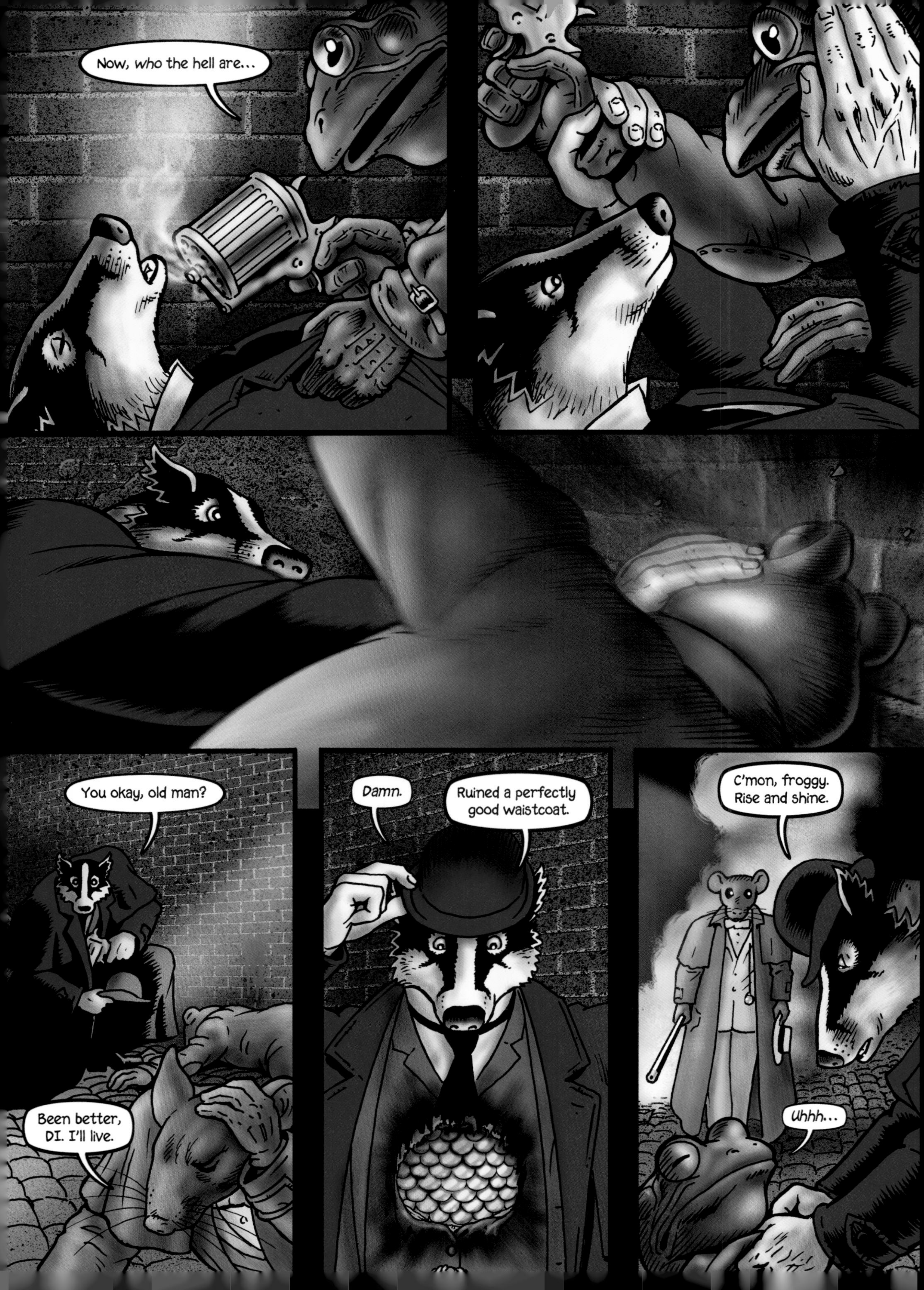
Now, who the hell are...
You okay, old man?
Been better, DI. I'll live.
Damn.
Ruined a perfectly good waistcoat.
C'mon, froggy. Rise and shine.
Uhhh...

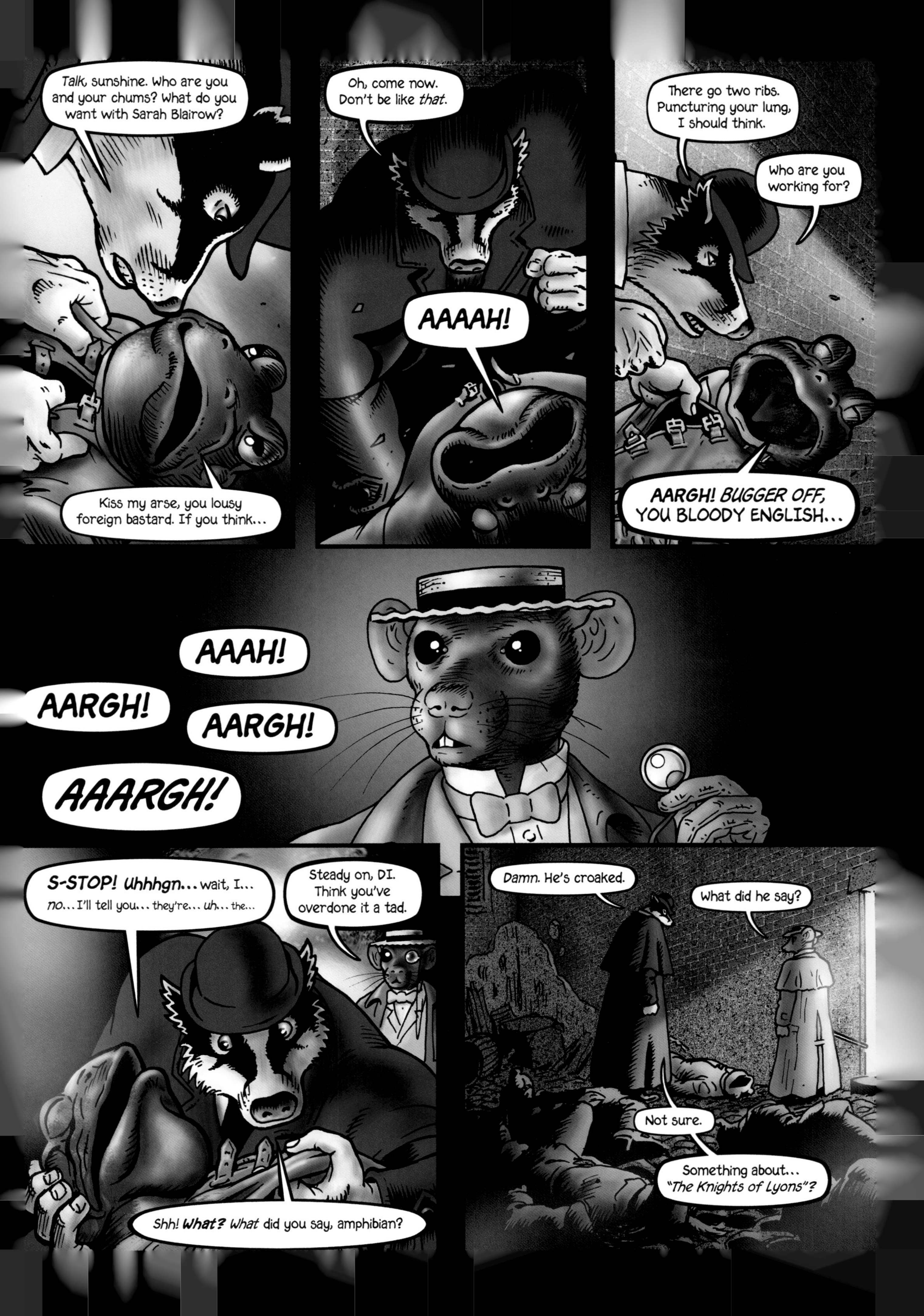

Talk, sunshine. Who are you and your chums? What do you want with Sarah Blairow?
Kiss my arse, you lousy foreign bastard. If you think...
Oh, come now. Don't be like *that.*
AAAAH!
There go two ribs. Puncturing your lung, I should think.
Who are you working for?
AARGH! *BUGGER OFF,* YOU BLOODY ENGLISH...
AAAH!
AARGH!
AARGH!
AAARGH!
S-STOP! Uhhhgn... wait, I... *no*... I'll tell you... they're... *uh*... the...
Steady on, DI. Think you've overdone it a tad.
Shh! ***What?*** *What* did you say, amphibian?
Damn. He's croaked.
What did he say?
Not sure.
Something about... *"The Knights of Lyons"*?

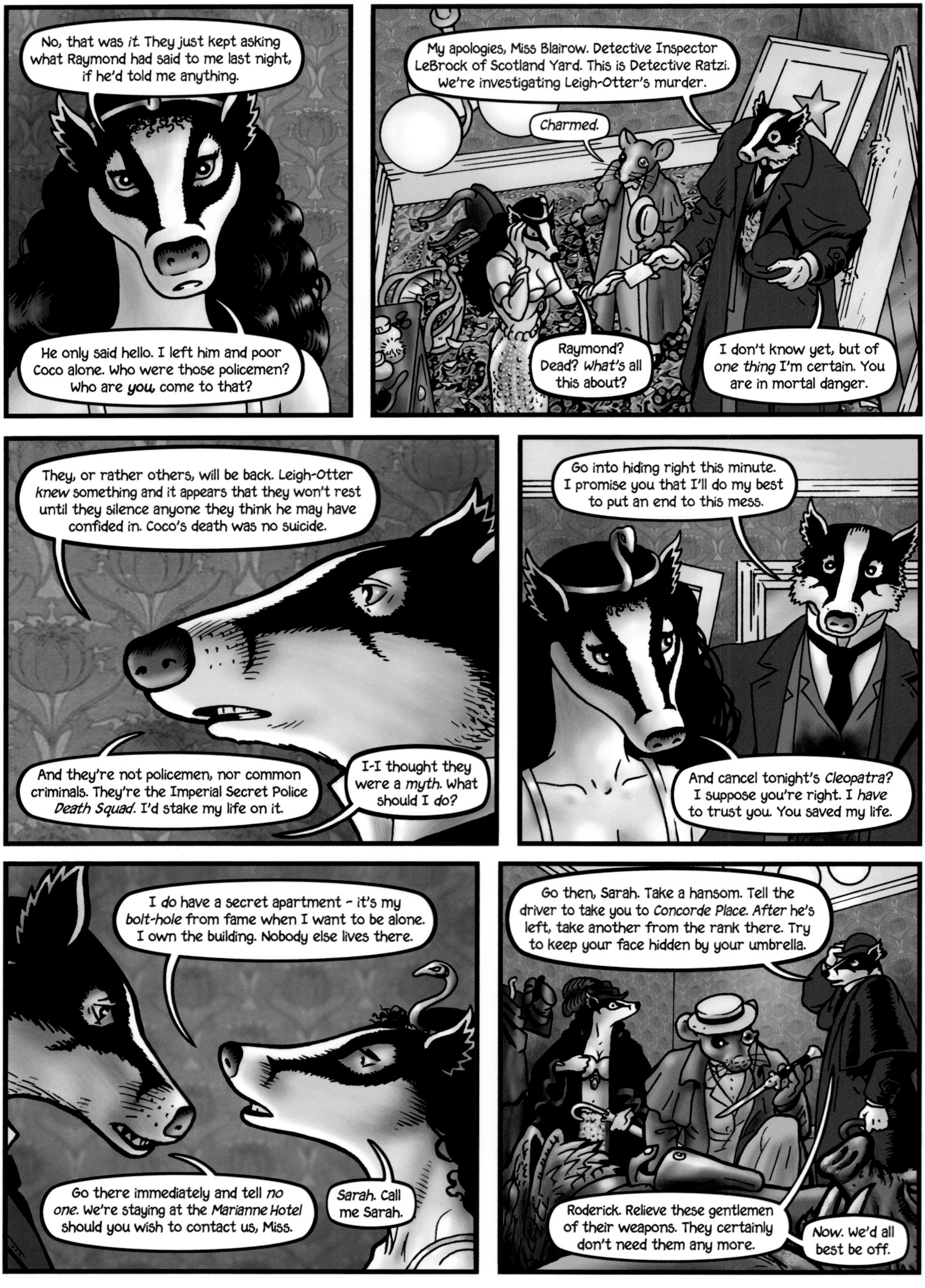

No, that was *it*. They just kept asking what Raymond had said to me last night, if he'd told me anything.
He only said hello. I left him and poor Coco alone. Who were those policemen? Who are **you**, come to that?
My apologies, Miss Blairow. Detective Inspector LeBrock of Scotland Yard. This is Detective Ratzi. We're investigating Leigh-Otter's murder.
Charmed.
Raymond? Dead? *What's* all this about?
I don't know yet, but of *one thing* I'm certain. You are in mortal danger.
They, or rather others, will be back. Leigh-Otter *knew* something and it appears that they won't rest until they silence anyone they think he may have confided in. Coco's death was no suicide.
And they're not policemen, nor common criminals. They're the Imperial Secret Police *Death Squad*. I'd stake my life on it.
I-I thought they were a *myth*. What should I *do?*
Go into hiding right this minute. I promise you that I'll do my best to put an end to this mess.
And cancel tonight's *Cleopatra?* I suppose you're right. I *have* to trust you. You saved my life.
I *do* have a secret apartment – it's my *bolt-hole* from fame when I want to be alone. I own the building. Nobody else lives there.
Go there immediately and tell *no one*. We're staying at the *Marianne Hotel* should you wish to contact us, Miss.
Sarah. Call me Sarah.
Go then, Sarah. Take a hansom. Tell the driver to take you to *Concorde Place*. *After* he's left, take another from the rank there. Try to keep your face hidden by your umbrella.
Roderick. Relieve these gentlemen of their weapons. They certainly don't need them any more.
Now. We'd all best be off.

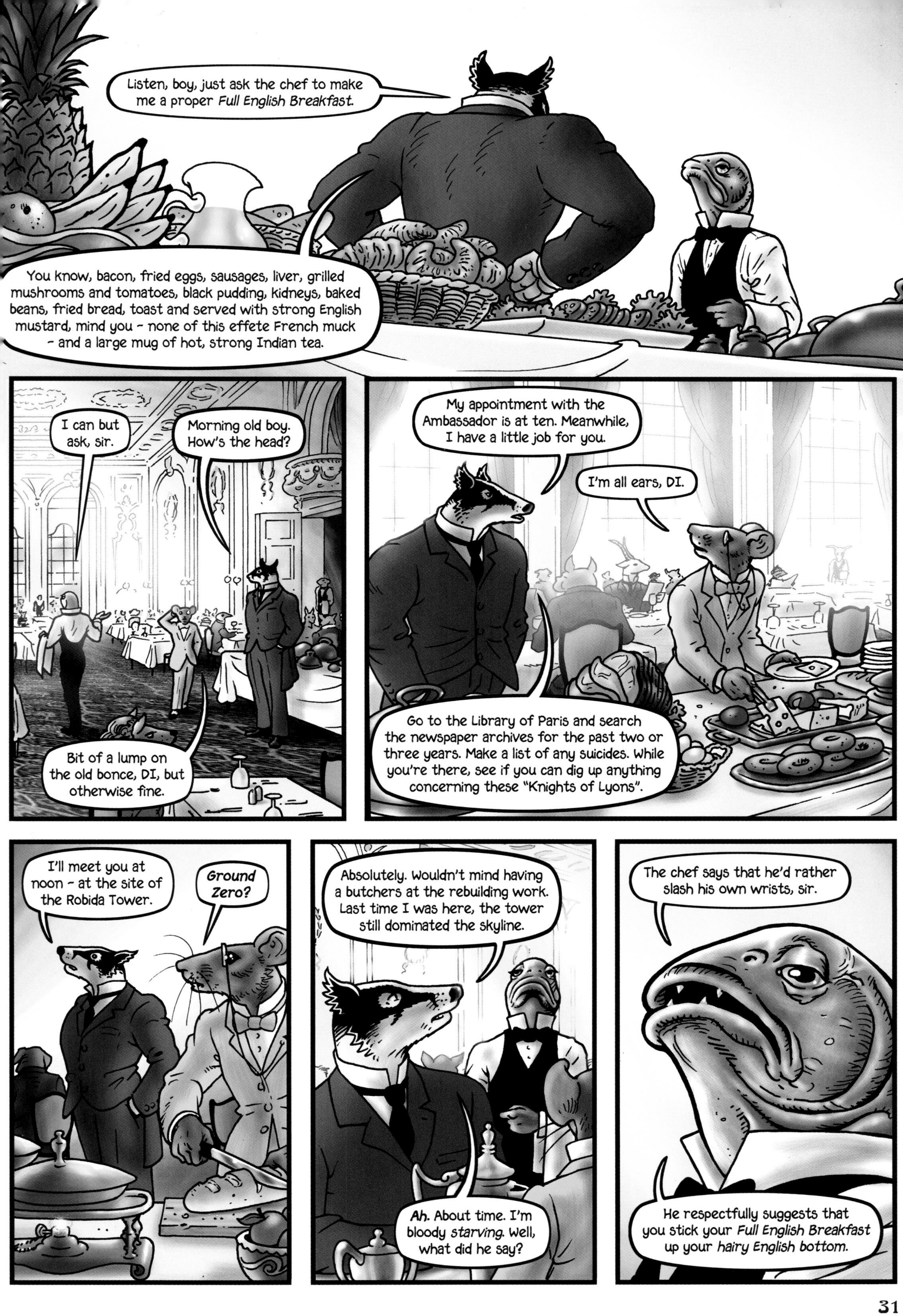
Listen, boy, just ask the chef to make me a proper *Full English Breakfast*.
You know, bacon, fried eggs, sausages, liver, grilled mushrooms and tomatoes, black pudding, kidneys, baked beans, fried bread, toast and served with strong English mustard, mind you - none of this effete French muck - and a large mug of hot, strong Indian tea.
I can but ask, sir.
Morning old boy. How's the head?
Bit of a lump on the old bonce, DI, but otherwise fine.
My appointment with the Ambassador is at ten. Meanwhile, I have a little job for you.
I'm all ears, DI.
Go to the Library of Paris and search the newspaper archives for the past two or three years. Make a list of any suicides. While you're there, see if you can dig up anything concerning these "Knights of Lyons".
I'll meet you at noon - at the site of the Robida Tower.
Ground Zero?
Absolutely. Wouldn't mind having a butchers at the rebuilding work. Last time I was here, the tower still dominated the skyline.
Ah. About time. I'm bloody *starving*. Well, what did he say?
The chef says that he'd rather slash his own wrists, sir.
He respectfully suggests that you stick your *Full English Breakfast* up your *hairy English bottom*.

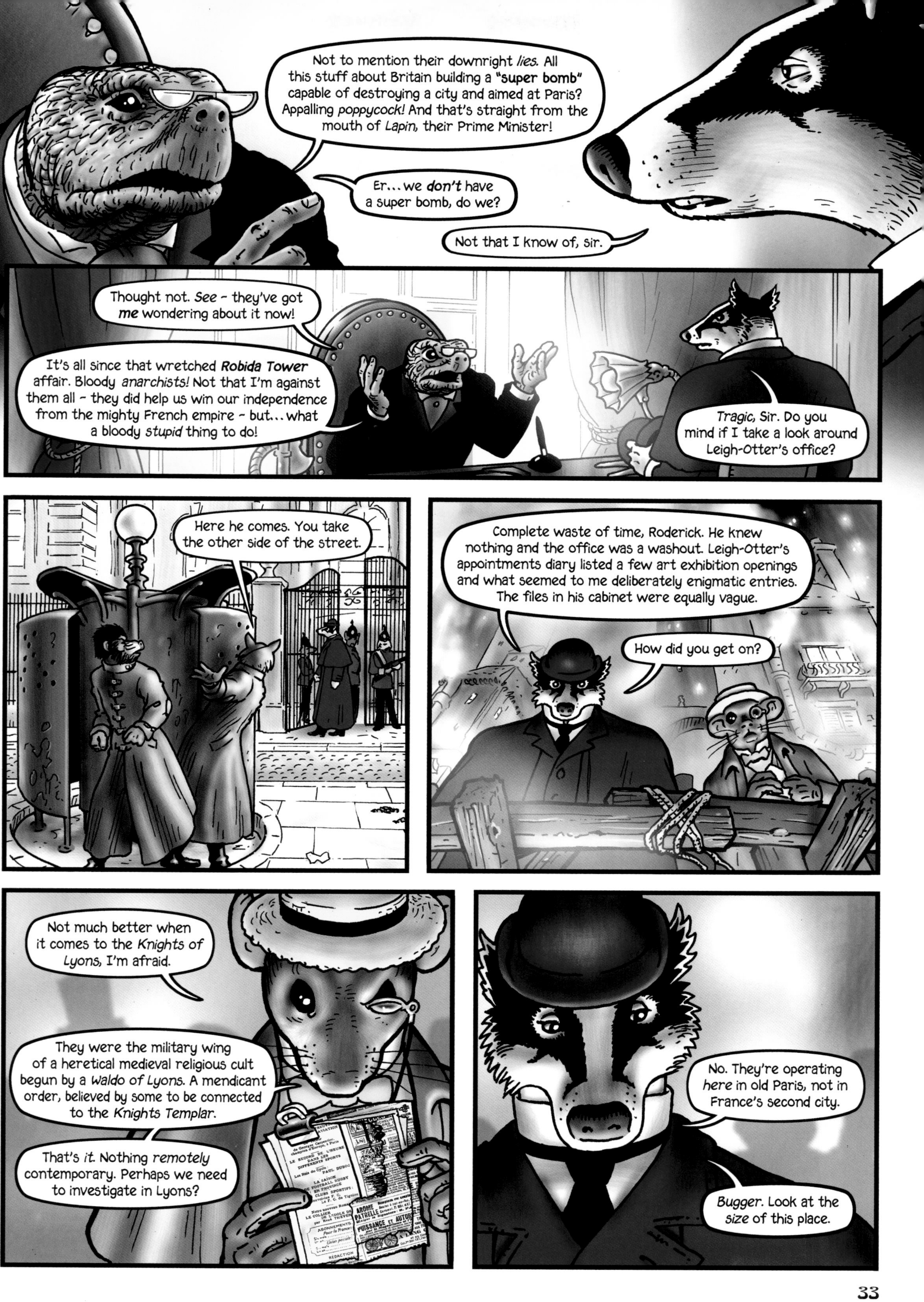

Not to mention their downright *lies*. All this stuff about Britain building a **"super bomb"** capable of destroying a city and aimed at Paris? Appalling *poppycock!* And that's straight from the mouth of *Lapin*, their Prime Minister!
Er... we **don't** have a super bomb, do we?
Not that I know of, sir.
Thought not. *See* – they've got **me** wondering about it now!
It's all since that wretched **Robida Tower** affair. Bloody *anarchists!* Not that I'm against them all – they did help us win our independence from the mighty French empire – but... what a bloody *stupid* thing to do!
Tragic, Sir. Do you mind if I take a look around Leigh-Otter's office?
Here he comes. You take the other side of the street.
Complete waste of time, Roderick. He knew nothing and the office was a washout. Leigh-Otter's appointments diary listed a few art exhibition openings and what seemed to me deliberately enigmatic entries. The files in his cabinet were equally vague.
How did you get on?
Not much better when it comes to the *Knights of Lyons*, I'm afraid.
They were the military wing of a heretical medieval religious cult begun by a *Waldo of Lyons*. A mendicant order, believed by some to be connected to the *Knights Templar*.
That's *it*. Nothing *remotely* contemporary. Perhaps we need to investigate in Lyons?
No. They're operating *here* in old Paris, not in France's second city.
Bugger. Look at the *size* of this place.

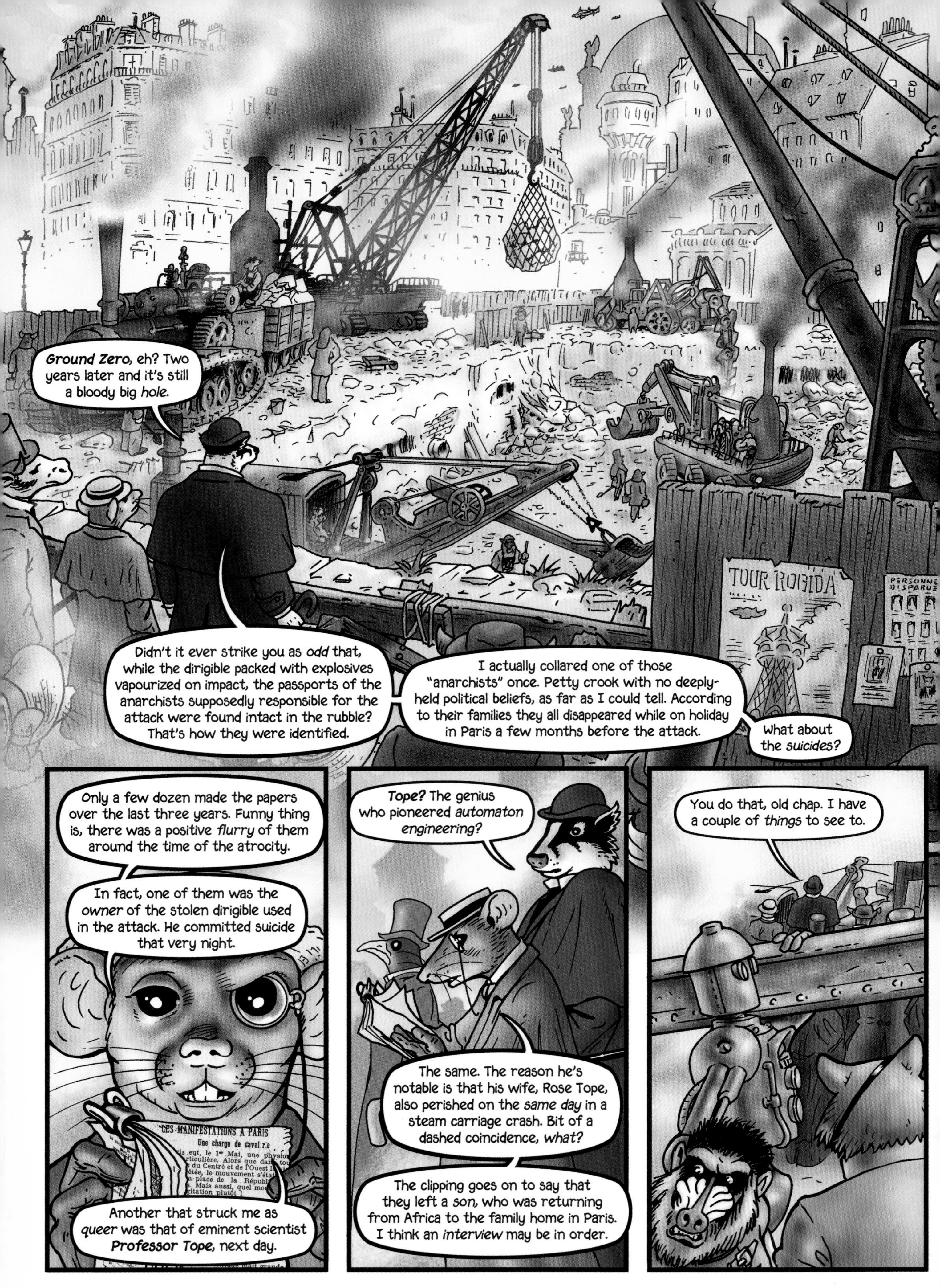
Ground Zero, eh? Two years later and it's still a bloody big hole.
TOUR ROBIDA
PERSONNES DISPARUES
Didn't it ever strike you as odd that, while the dirigible packed with explosives vapourized on impact, the passports of the anarchists supposedly responsible for the attack were found intact in the rubble? That's how they were identified.
I actually collared one of those "anarchists" once. Petty crook with no deeply-held political beliefs, as far as I could tell. According to their families they all disappeared while on holiday in Paris a few months before the attack.
What about the suicides?
Only a few dozen made the papers over the last three years. Funny thing is, there was a positive flurry of them around the time of the atrocity.
In fact, one of them was the owner of the stolen dirigible used in the attack. He committed suicide that very night.
LES MANIFESTATIONS A PARIS
Another that struck me as queer was that of eminent scientist Professor Tope, next day.
Tope? The genius who pioneered automaton engineering?
The same. The reason he's notable is that his wife, Rose Tope, also perished on the same day in a steam carriage crash. Bit of a dashed coincidence, what?
The clipping goes on to say that they left a son, who was returning from Africa to the family home in Paris. I think an interview may be in order.
You do that, old chap. I have a couple of things to see to.

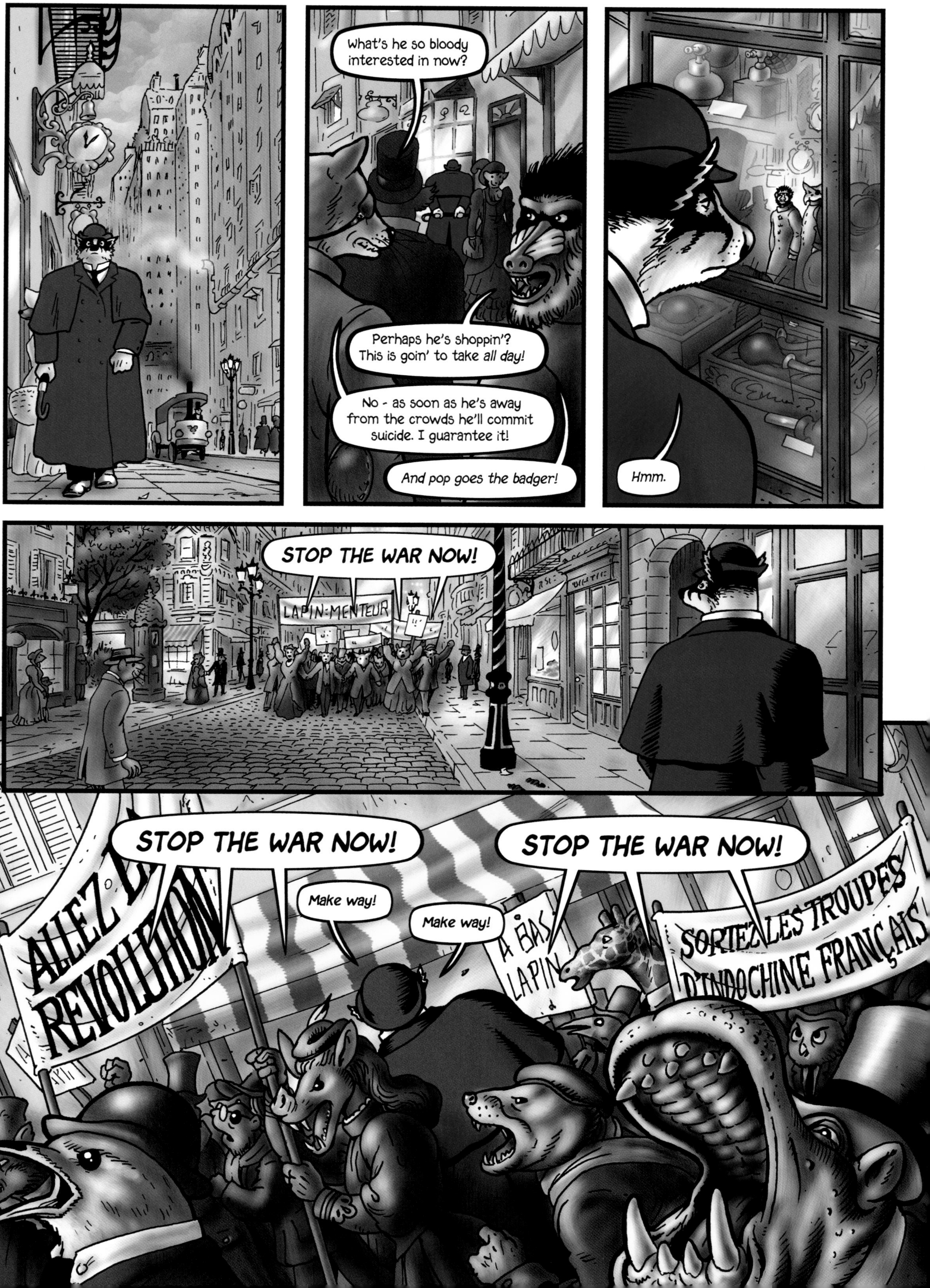
What's he so bloody interested in now?
Perhaps he's shoppin'? This is goin' to take *all day!*
No - as soon as he's away from the crowds he'll commit suicide. I guarantee it!
And pop goes the badger!
Hmm.
STOP THE WAR NOW!
LAPIN:MENTEUR
STOP THE WAR NOW!
STOP THE WAR NOW!
ALLEZ
REVOLUTION
Make way!
Make way!
A BAS LAPIN
SORTIEZ LES TROUPES D'INDOCHINE FRANÇAIS

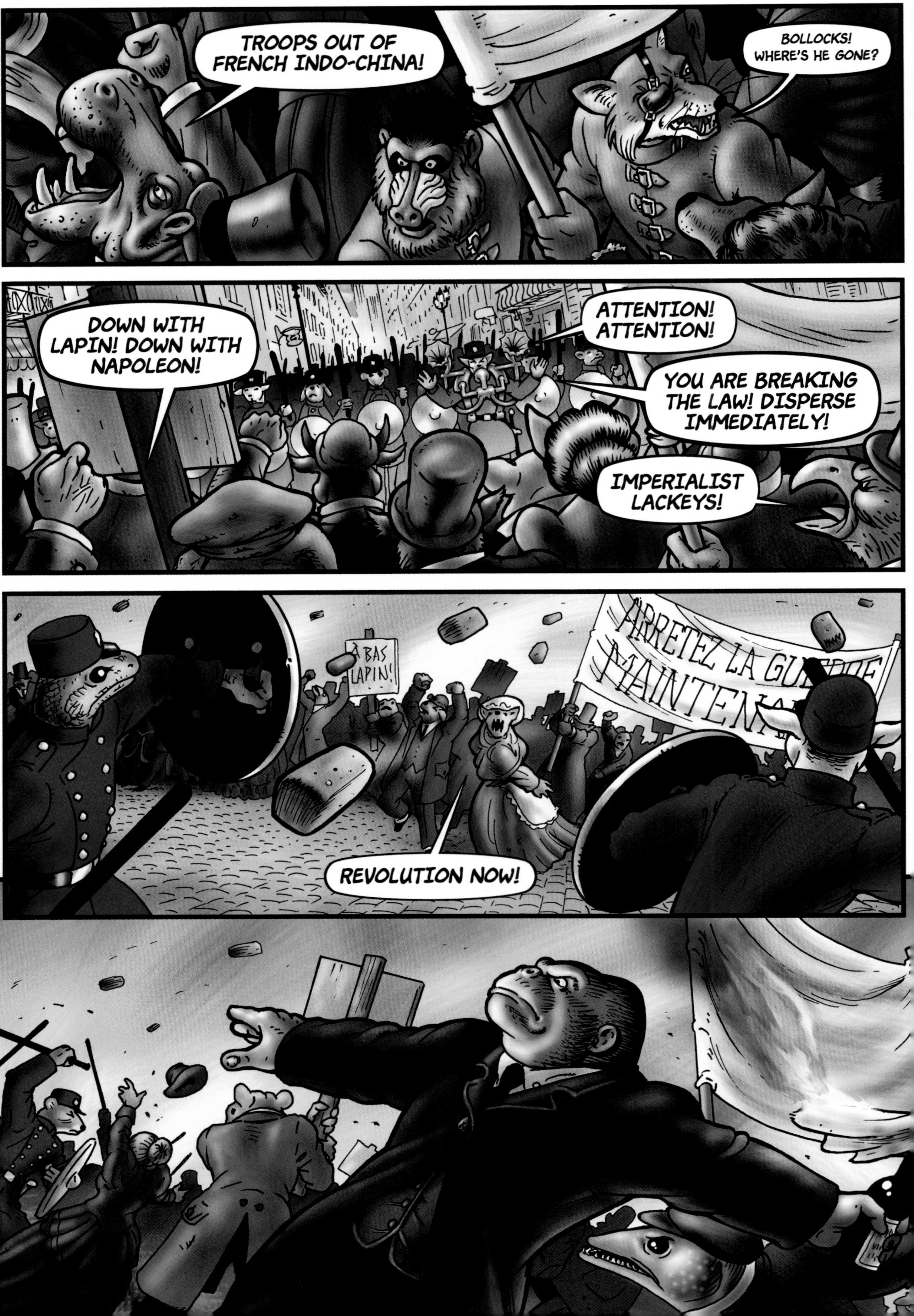
TROOPS OUT OF FRENCH INDO-CHINA!
BOLLOCKS! WHERE'S HE GONE?
DOWN WITH LAPIN! DOWN WITH NAPOLEON!
ATTENTION! ATTENTION!
YOU ARE BREAKING THE LAW! DISPERSE IMMEDIATELY!
IMPERIALIST LACKEYS!
À BAS LAPIN!
REVOLUTION NOW!

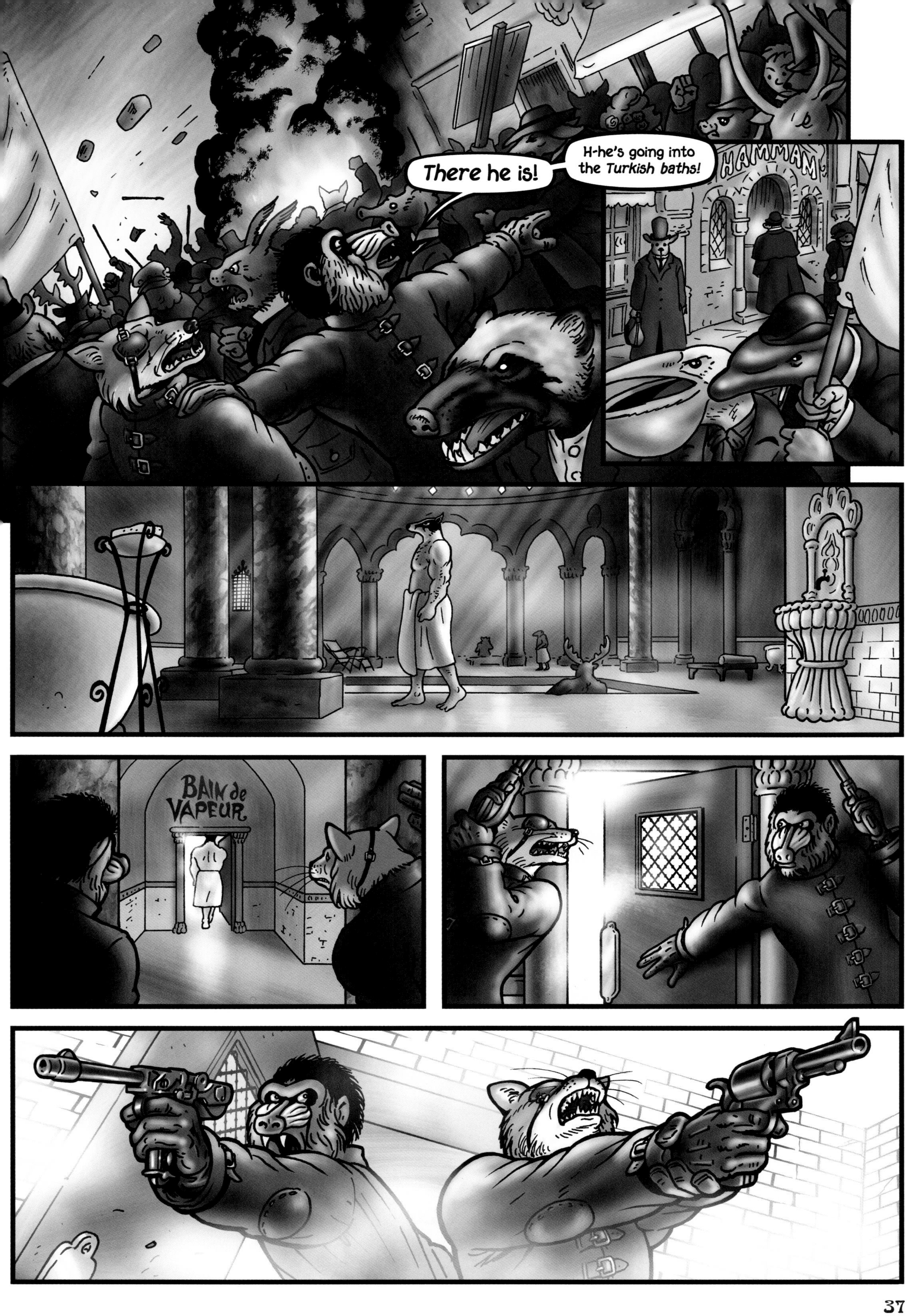
There he is!
H-he's going into the *Turkish* baths!
BAIN de VAPEUR

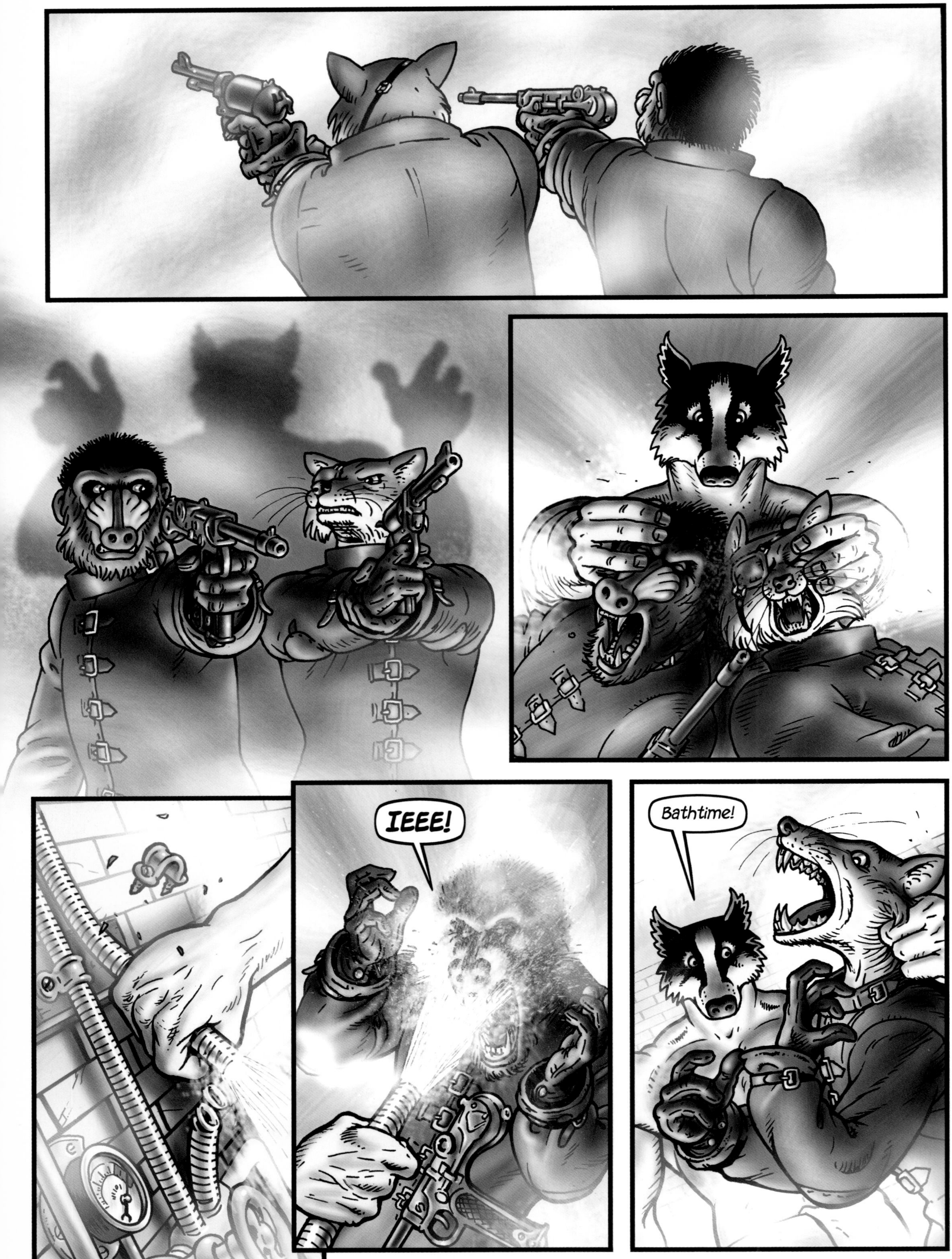
IEEE!
Bathtime!

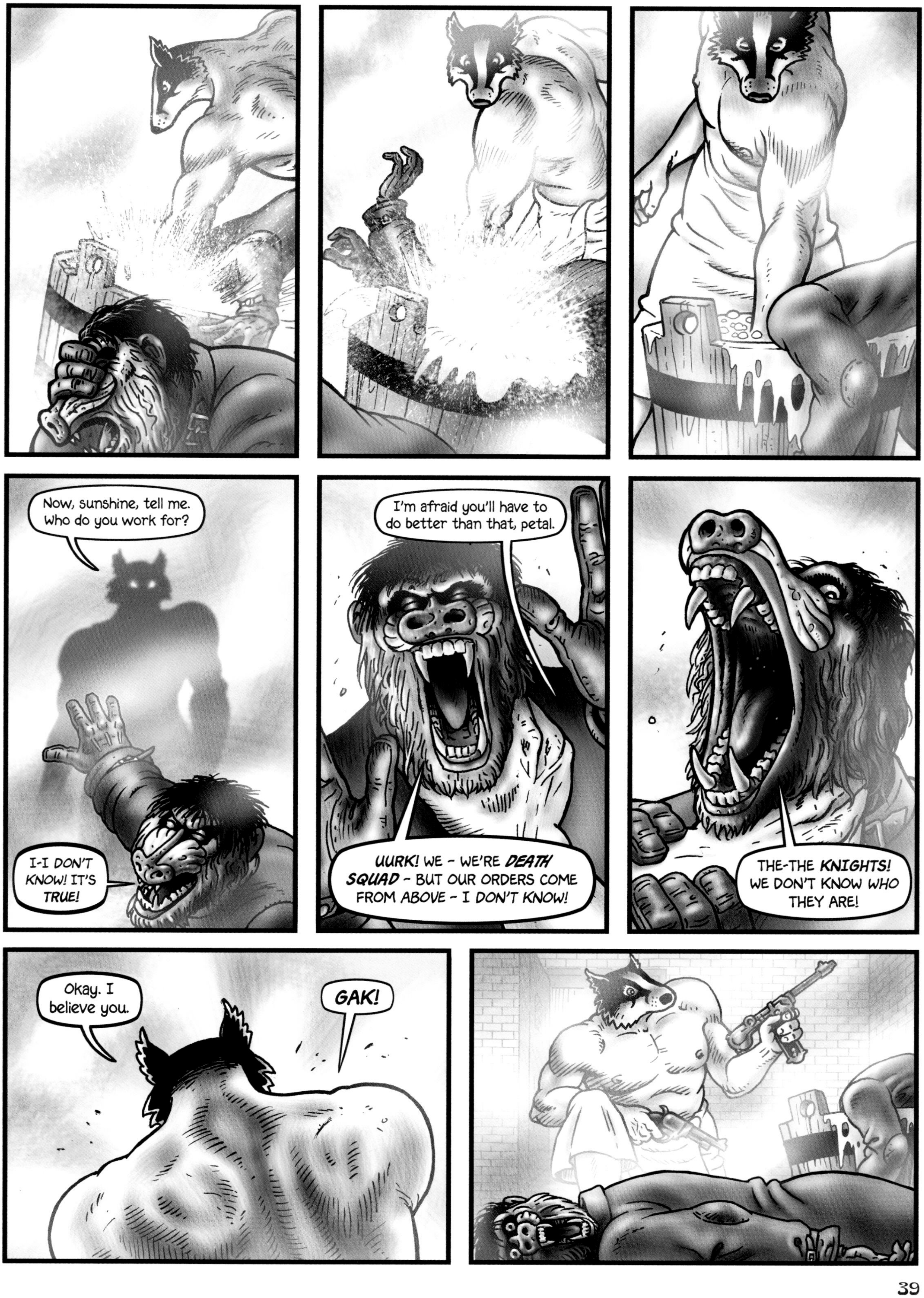
Now, sunshine, tell me. Who do you work for?
I-I DON'T KNOW! IT'S TRUE!
I'm afraid you'll have to do better than that, petal.
UURK! WE - WE'RE DEATH SQUAD - BUT OUR ORDERS COME FROM ABOVE - I DON'T KNOW!
THE-THE KNIGHTS! WE DON'T KNOW WHO THEY ARE!
Okay. I believe you.
GAK!

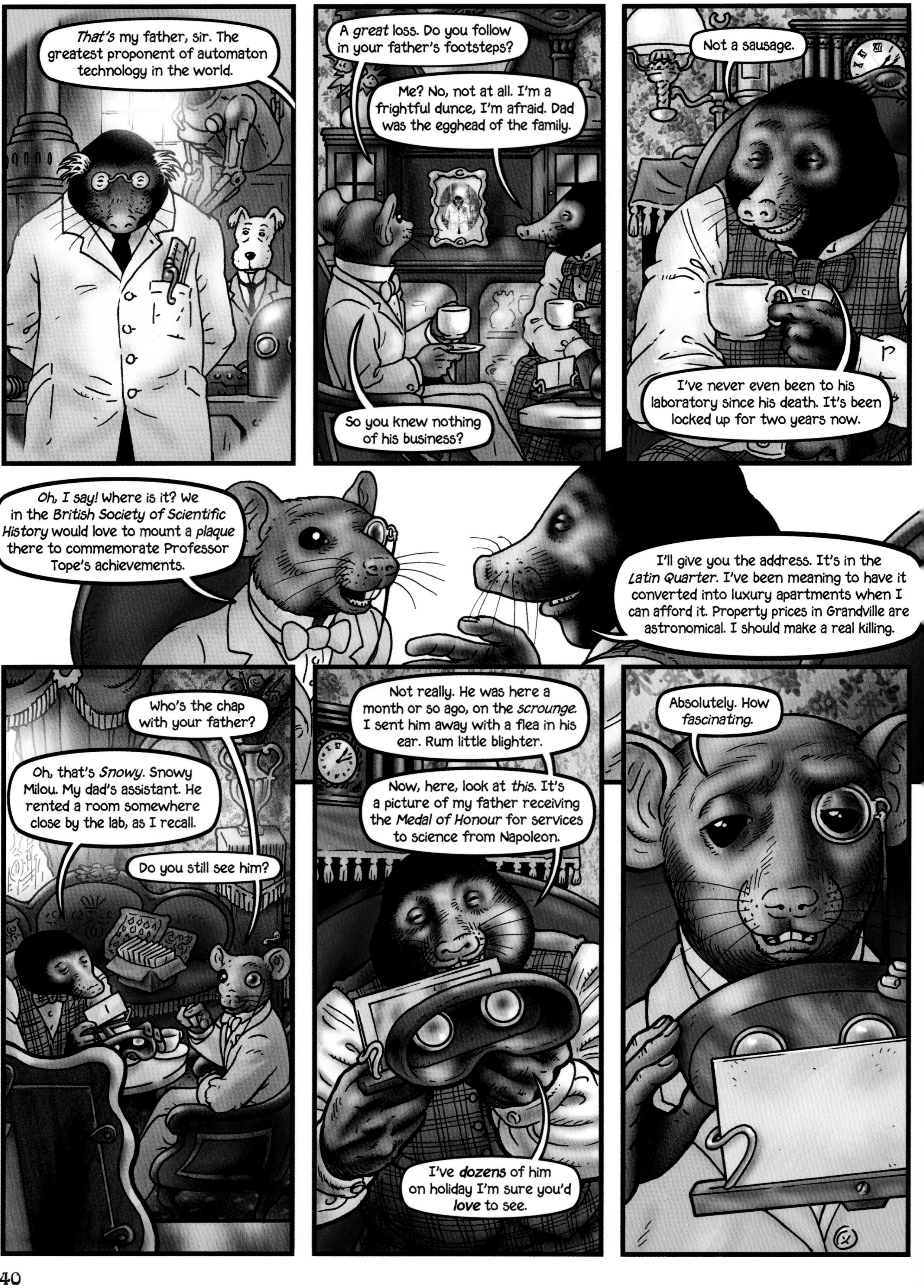
That's my father, sir. The greatest proponent of automaton technology in the world.
A *great* loss. Do you follow in your father's footsteps?
Me? No, not at all. I'm a frightful dunce, I'm afraid. Dad was the egghead of the family.
So you knew nothing of his business?
Not a sausage.
I've never even been to his laboratory since his death. It's been locked up for two years now.
Oh, I say! Where is it? We in the *British Society of Scientific History* would love to mount a *plaque* there to commemorate Professor Tope's achievements.
I'll give you the address. It's in the *Latin Quarter*. I've been meaning to have it converted into luxury apartments when I can afford it. Property prices in Grandville are astronomical. I should make a real killing.
Who's the chap with your father?
Oh, that's *Snowy*. Snowy Milou. My dad's assistant. He rented a room somewhere close by the lab, as I recall.
Do you still see him?
Not really. He was here a month or so ago, on the *scrounge*. I sent him away with a flea in his ear. Rum little blighter.
Now, here, look at *this*. It's a picture of my father receiving the *Medal of Honour* for services to science from Napoleon.
I've **dozens** of him on holiday I'm sure you'd **love** to see.
Absolutely. How *fascinating*.

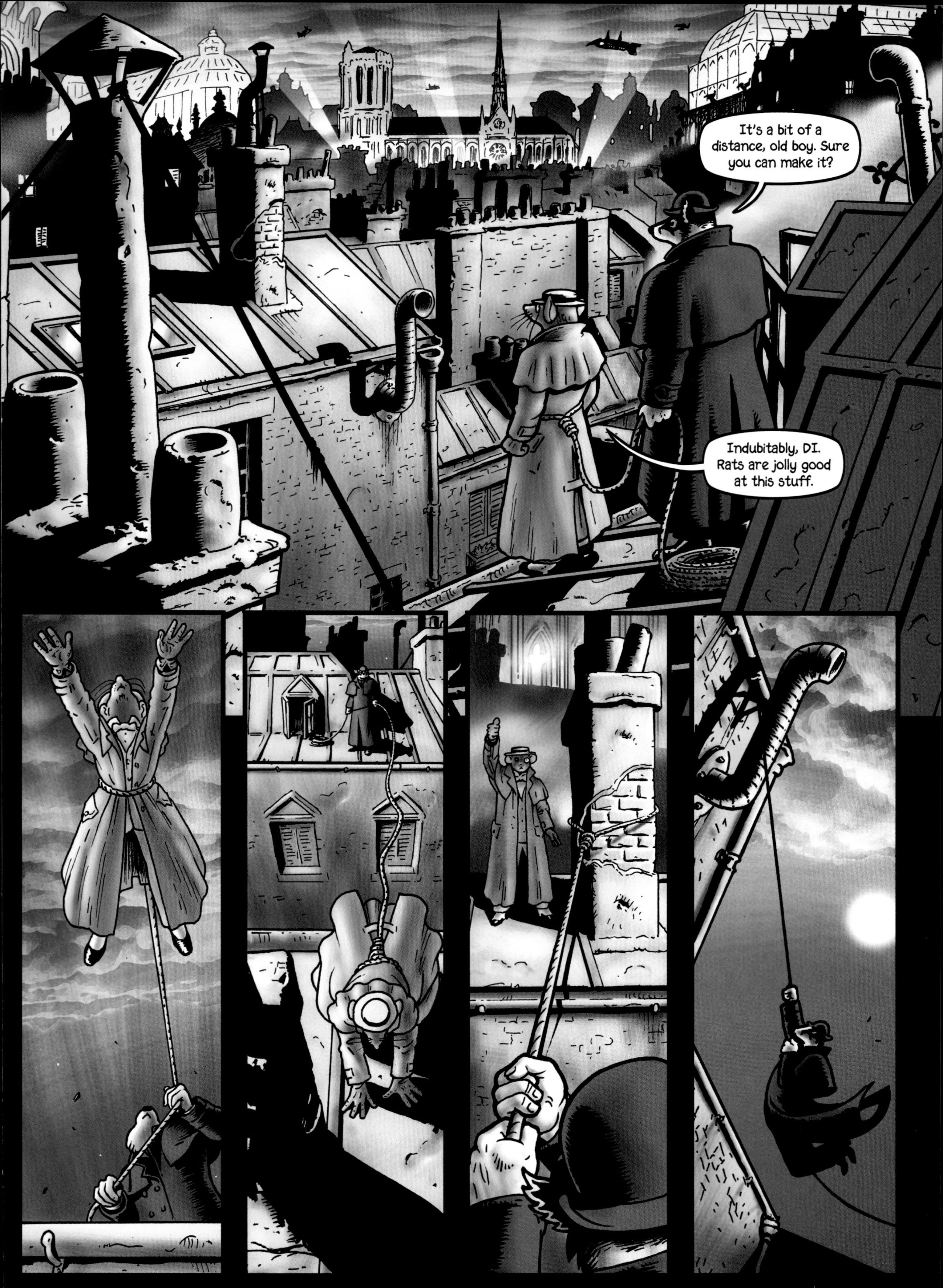
It's a bit of a distance, old boy. Sure you can make it?
Indubitably, DI. Rats are jolly good at this stuff.

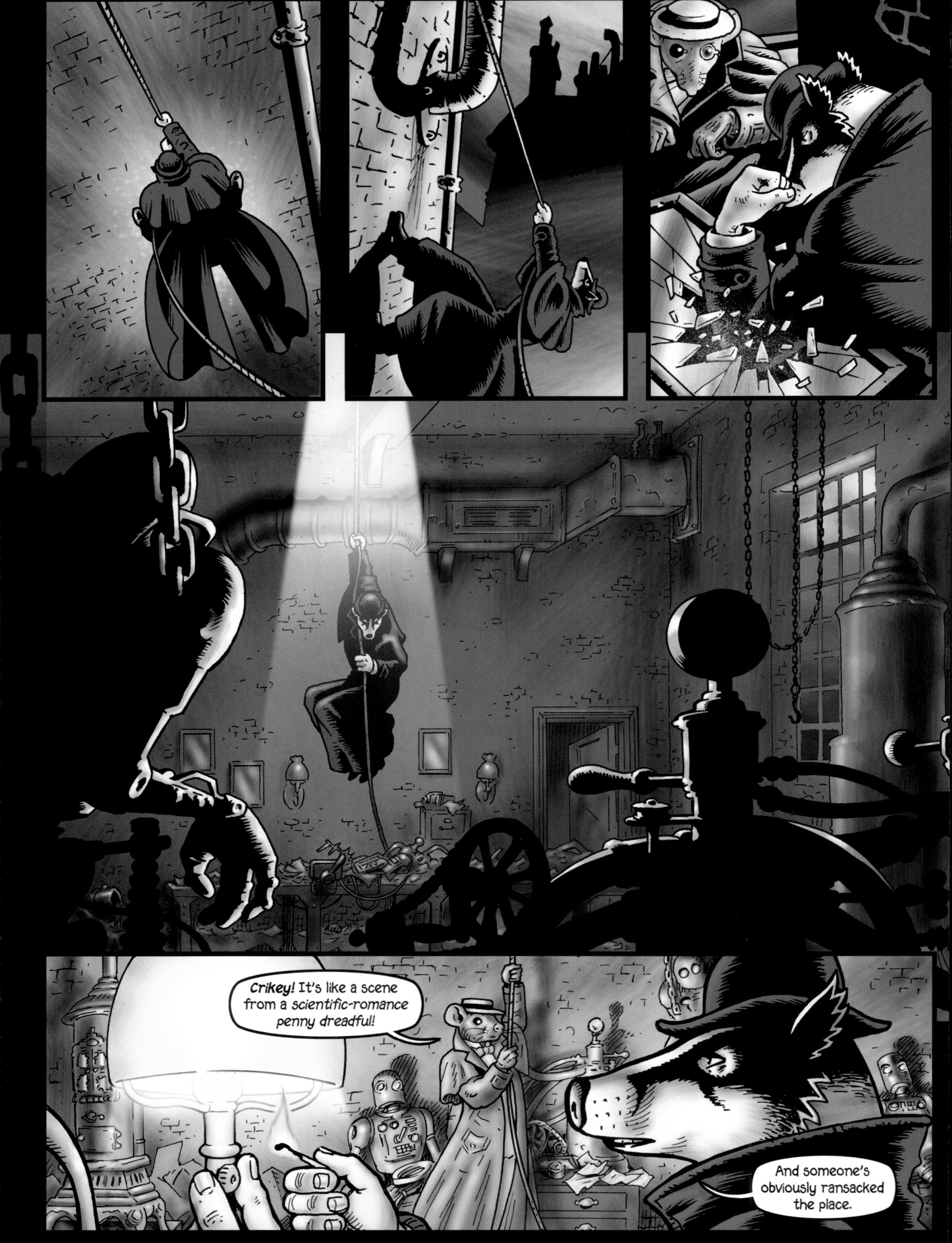
Crikey! It's like a scene from a *scientific-romance penny dreadful!*
And someone's obviously ransacked the place.

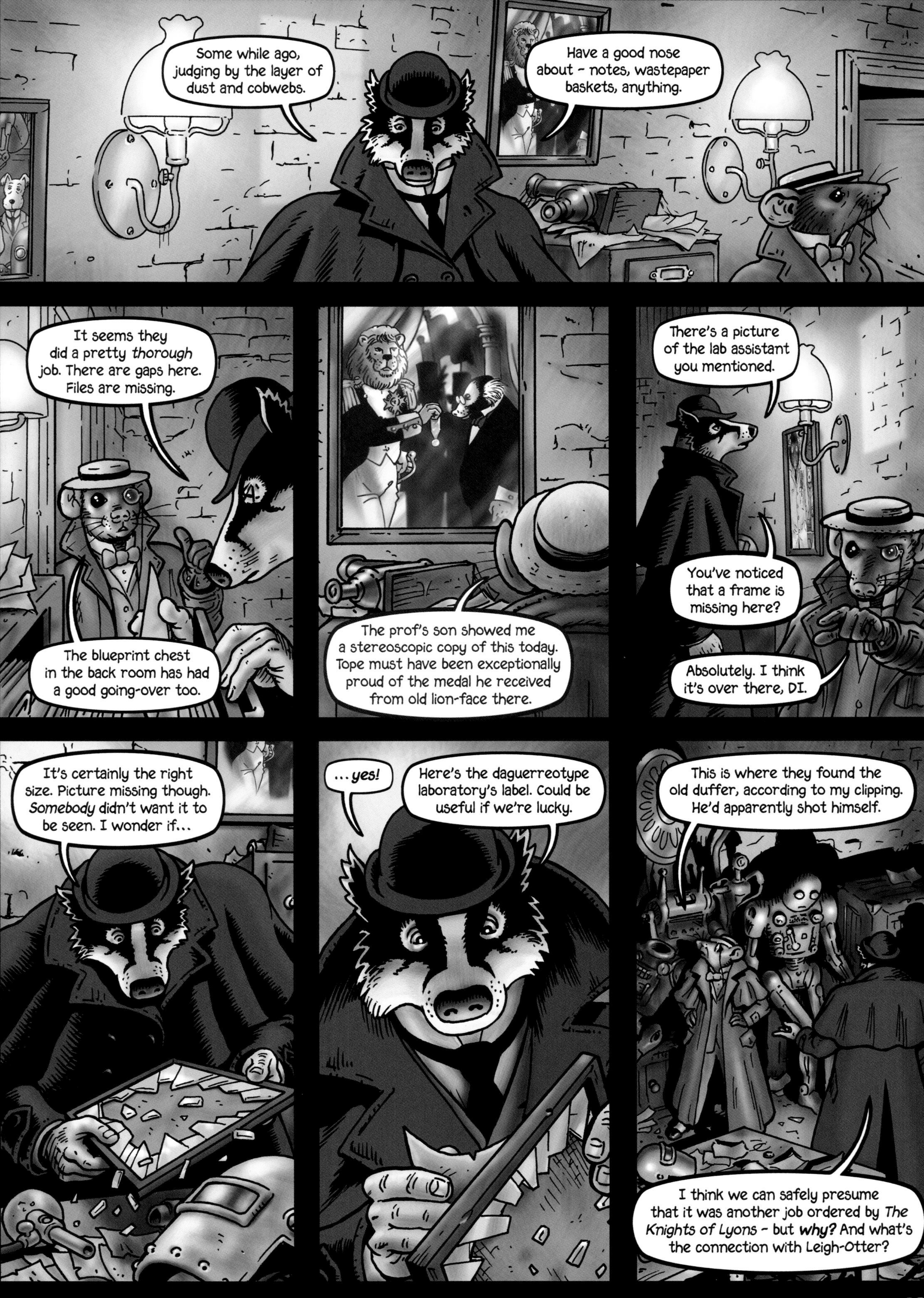
Some while ago, judging by the layer of dust and cobwebs.
Have a good nose about – notes, wastepaper baskets, anything.
It seems they did a pretty *thorough* job. There are gaps here. Files are missing.
The blueprint chest in the back room has had a good going-over too.
The prof's son showed me a stereoscopic copy of this today. Tope must have been exceptionally proud of the medal he received from old lion-face there.
There's a picture of the lab assistant you mentioned.
You've noticed that a frame is missing here?
Absolutely. I think it's over there, DI.
It's certainly the right size. Picture missing though. *Somebody* didn't want it to be seen. I wonder if...
... *yes!*
Here's the daguerreotype laboratory's label. Could be useful if we're lucky.
This is where they found the old duffer, according to my clipping. He'd apparently shot himself.
I think we can safely presume that it was another job ordered by *The Knights of Lyons* – but ***why?*** And what's the connection with Leigh-Otter?

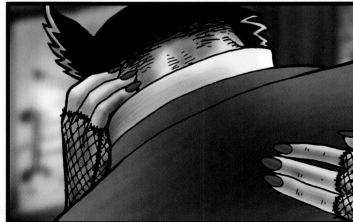

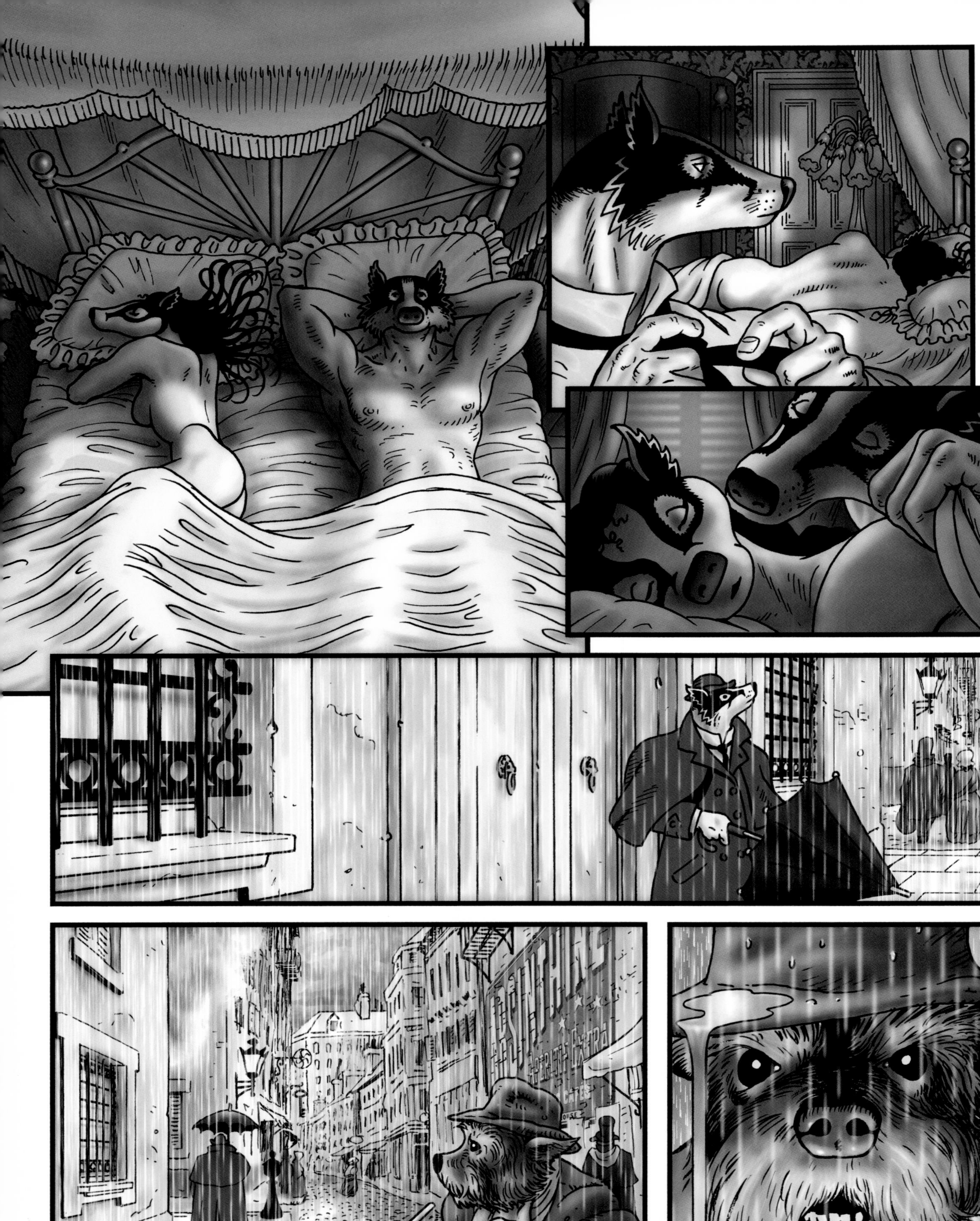

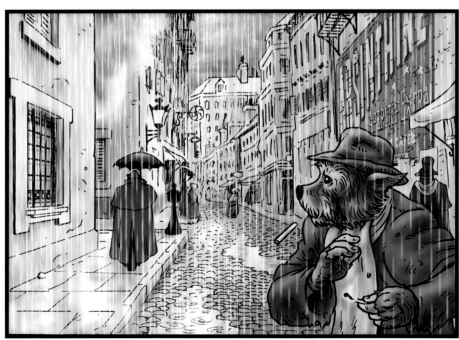

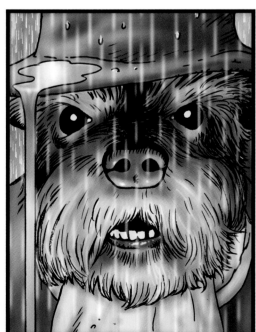

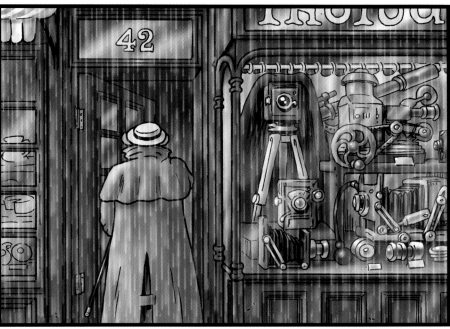

49

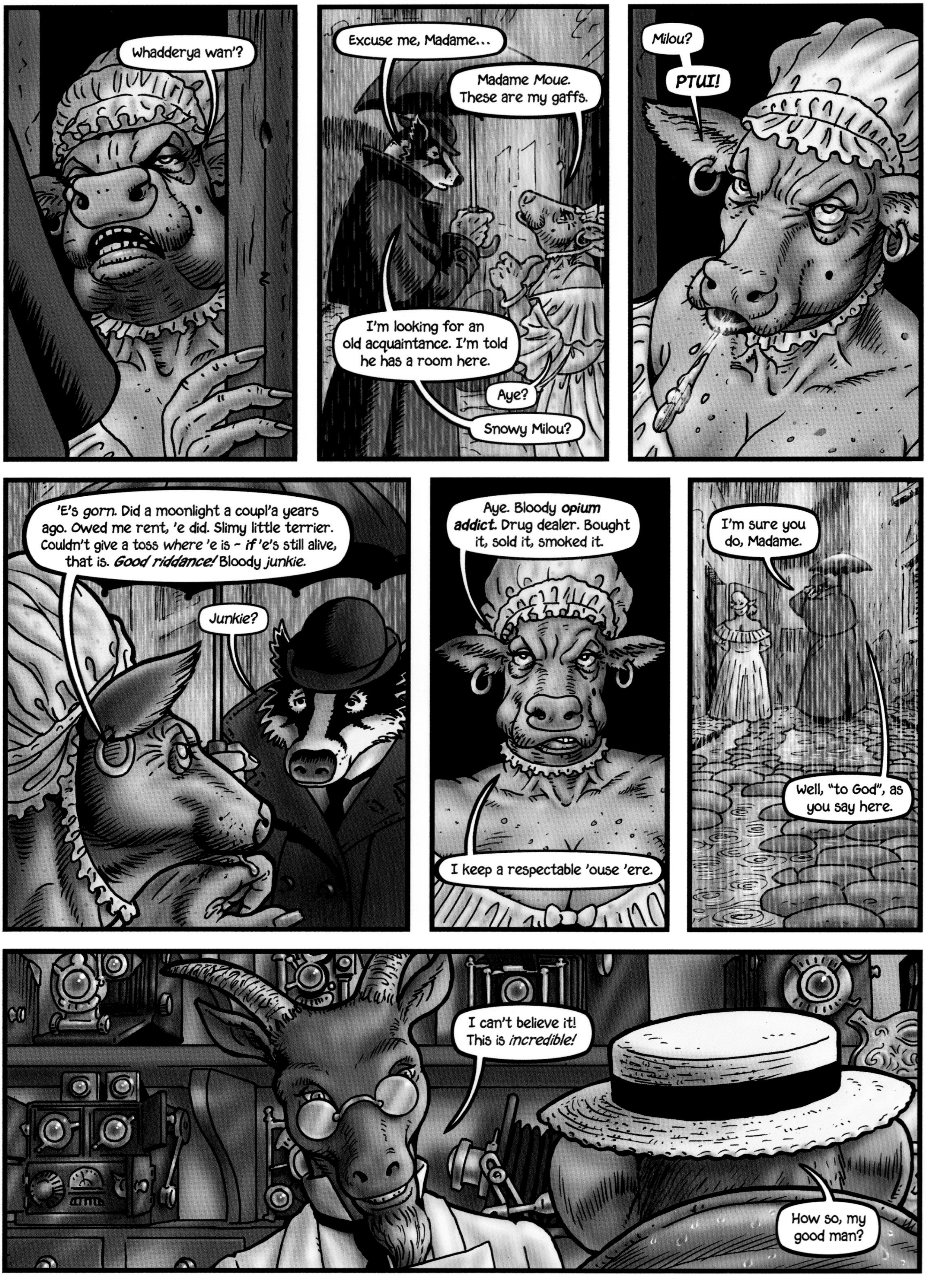
Whadderya wan'?
Excuse me, Madame...
Madame Moue. These are my gaffs.
I'm looking for an old acquaintance. I'm told he has a room here.
Aye?
Snowy Milou?
Milou?
PTUI!
'E's gorn. Did a moonlight a coupl'a years ago. Owed me rent, 'e did. Slimy little terrier. Couldn't give a toss where 'e is – if 'e's still alive, that is. Good riddance! Bloody junkie.
Junkie?
Aye. Bloody opium addict. Drug dealer. Bought it, sold it, smoked it.
I keep a respectable 'ouse 'ere.
I'm sure you do, Madame.
Well, "to God", as you say here.
I can't believe it! This is incredible!
How so, my good man?

Why, all of these people are *famous!*

Look, here's Professor Tope! And the Prime Minister! The War Minister! The Archbishop of Paris! The Chief of Police! And Madame Krupp herself!

What an *illustrious* hunting party!

If you say so, old bean. How much do I owe you?

This is very interesting.

I take it you noticed the year on the label from the picture frame?

Absolutely, DI. Two years ago.

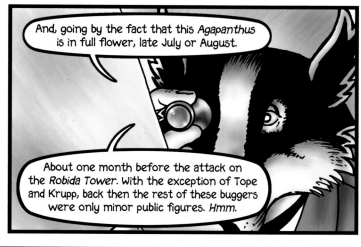

And, going by the fact that this *Agapanthus* is in full flower, late July or August.

About one month before the attack on the *Robida Tower*. With the exception of Tope and Krupp, back then the rest of these buggers were only minor public figures. *Hmm.*

Jean-Marie Lapin, now the Prime Minister, was simply the leader of a marginal far-right nationalist party. He shot to power in the elections following the Robida outrage – a landslide victory. What he promised was a "War on Terror" and a hard line against "British Anarchy".

His first act as PM was to appoint these three to key posts and pass several acts drastically curtailing civil liberties. Last year, he declared war on the *Communards* in French Indo-China.

But what does *this* have to do with Leigh-Otter, DI?

As a diplomat, he would have probably met one or more of them.

The Death Squad is a branch of the Secret Police. The Hyena there is their boss. I'll lay odds here are our *Knights of Lyons*.

Which do you think is the weakest link?

Let's start with the primate...

...after I've had a little talk with André Pegasus – *The Drug Baron of Paris.*

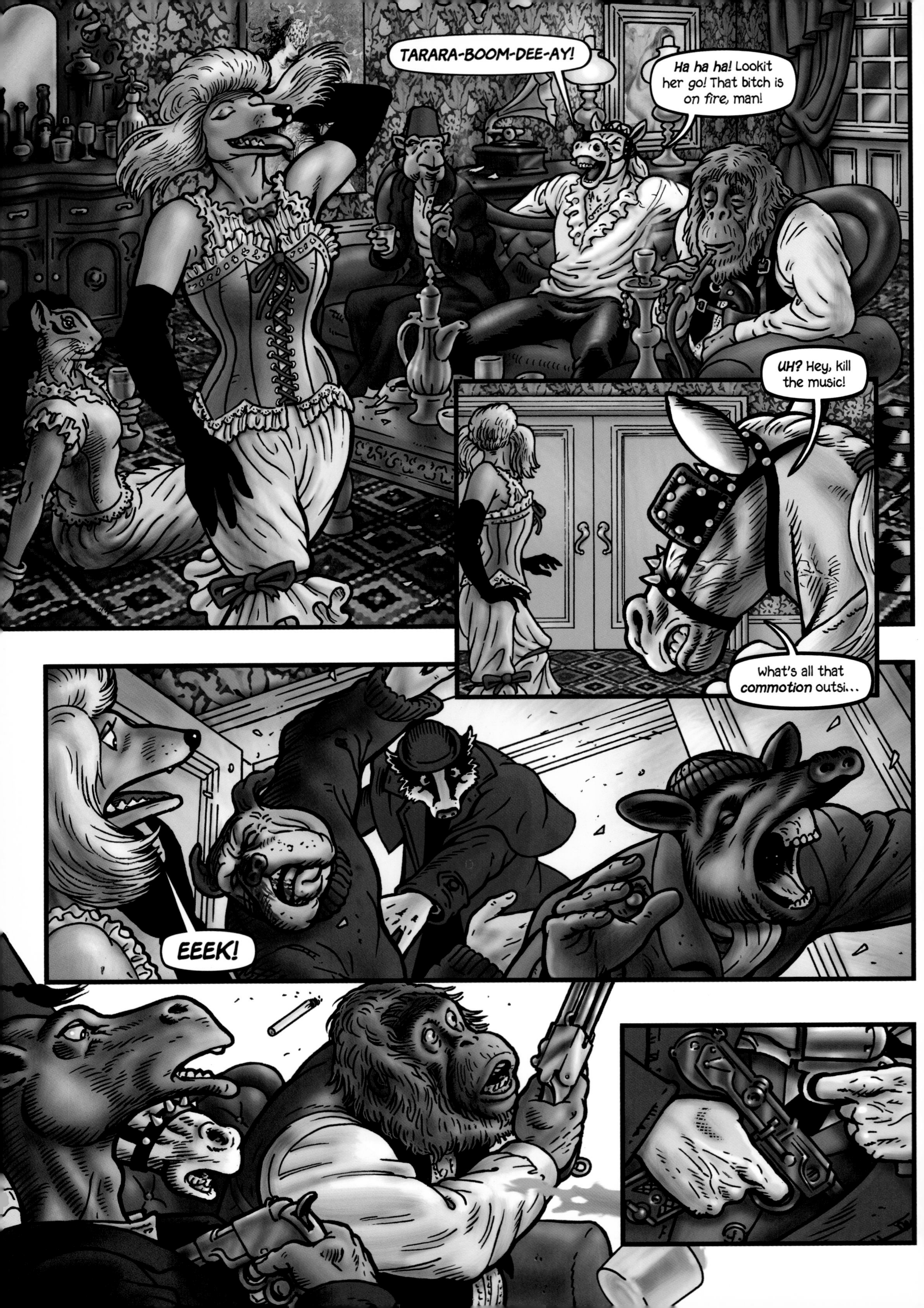
TARARA-BOOM-DEE-AY!
Ha ha ha! Lookit her go! That bitch is on fire, man!
UH? Hey, kill the music!
What's all that commotion outsi...
EEEK!

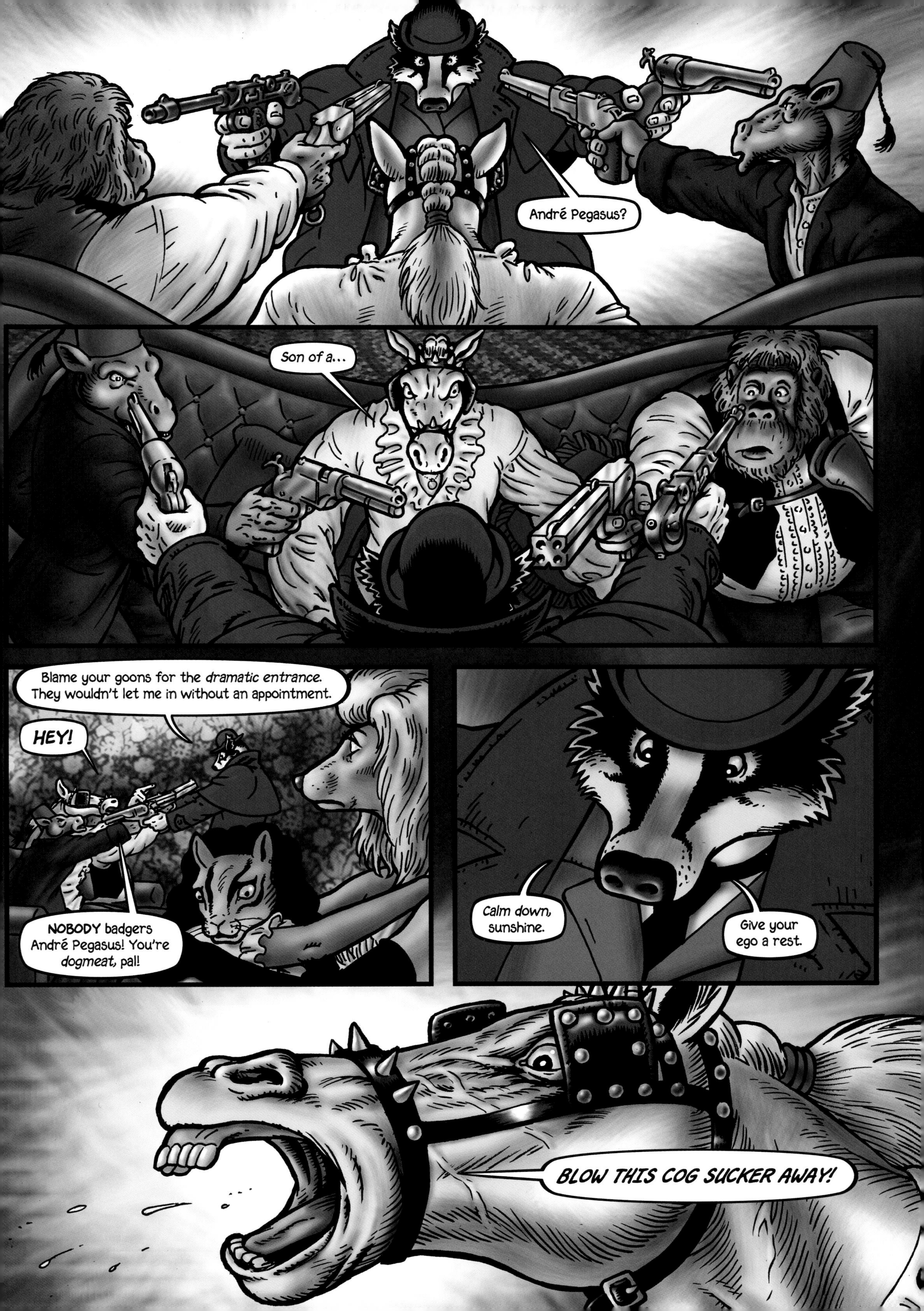

André Pegasus?
Son of a...
Blame your goons for the *dramatic entrance*. They wouldn't let me in without an appointment.
HEY!
NOBODY badgers André Pegasus! You're *dogmeat*, pal!
Calm down, sunshine.
Give your ego a rest.
BLOW THIS COG SUCKER AWAY!

54

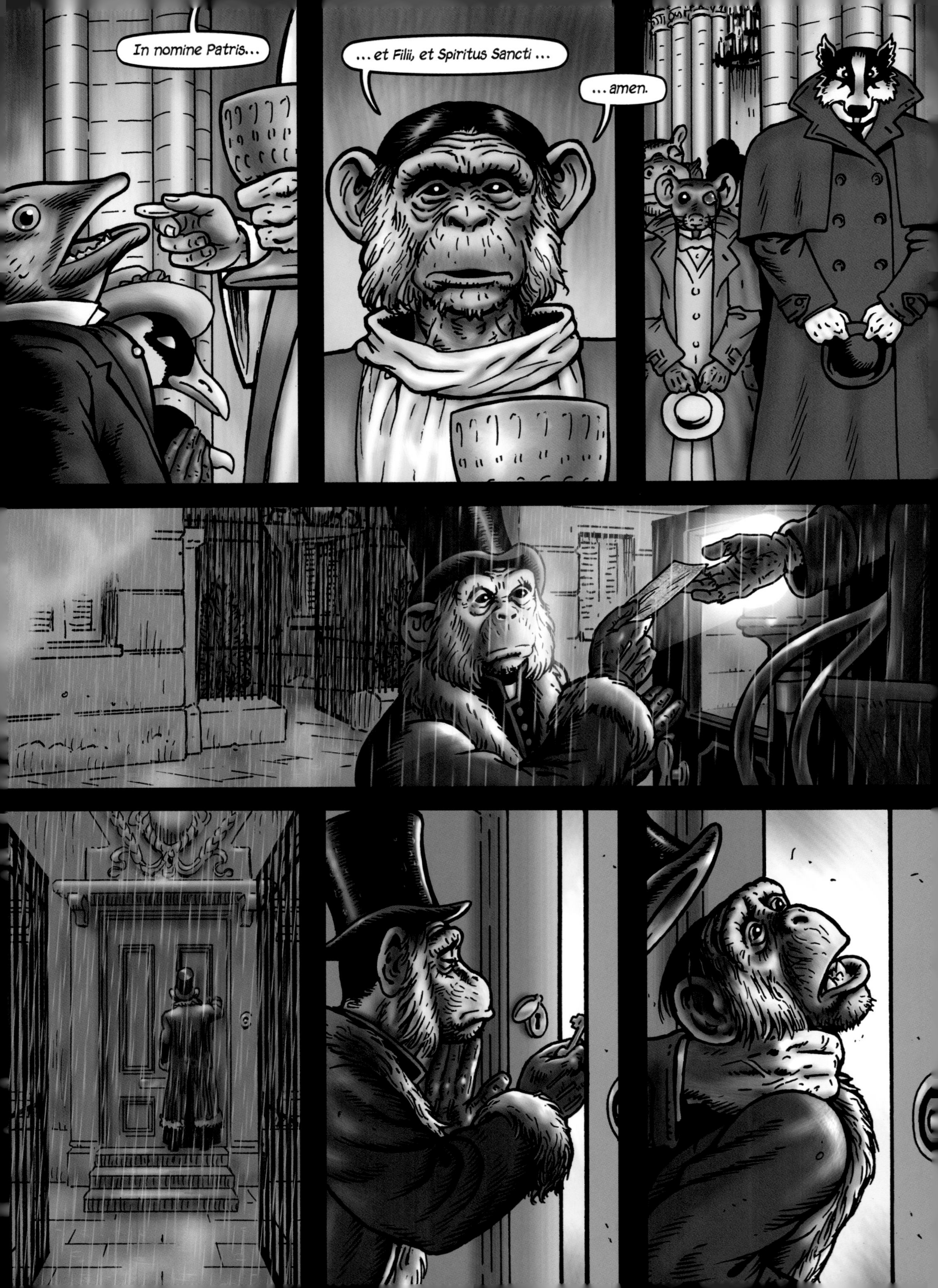
In nomine Patris...
... et Filii, et Spiritus Sancti ...
... amen.

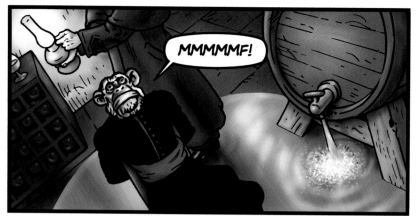

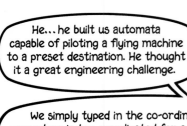

He...he built us automata capable of piloting a flying machine to a preset destination. He thought it a great engineering challenge.

We simply typed in the co-ordinates. Take-off procedure is too complicated for a machine though – too many *variables* of wind speed and steam pressure and other things I know nothing about.

That's why we needed a *pilot*. We paid the owner of the dirigible to get it into the air, power up the automaton and bail out.

Then had him killed the same night.

He couldn't be trusted. It was essential that the *anarchists* were blamed for the attack – if not it would have all been for nothing. Some *sacrifices* had to be made for the greater good.

Why kill Tope?

After the attack, he put two and two together and realized he'd been used. The fool wanted to turn himself in. We couldn't allow that.

Of course not. Well, your plan worked.

The nationalist vote swept Lapin to victory in the election just a few weeks later.

But it wasn't *enough!* We had to rig the election – even though Krupp's newspapers made him appear to be the popular choice. Look, untie me. That's all I know, I swear to God.

How did Leigh-Otter become involved?

He...he was discovered eavesdropping on a meeting we had in Paris last Monday. He escaped and took off in a cab, chased by Hyen's underlings. That's all I know.

I'm a *man of God!* I've nothing to do with *violence! Let me go!*

You know a *lot* more than that, I'm sure. What are the Knights' plans? *What* are they plotting next?

I've *told* you! I don't know *anything!*

You *must* know. You're one of them.

Tell me!

GO TO HELL!

Listen, sunshine, I'm running out of *patience.* I'm going to start with your *ears,* then your *fingers,* then your *eyes.* Just tell me your plans.

63

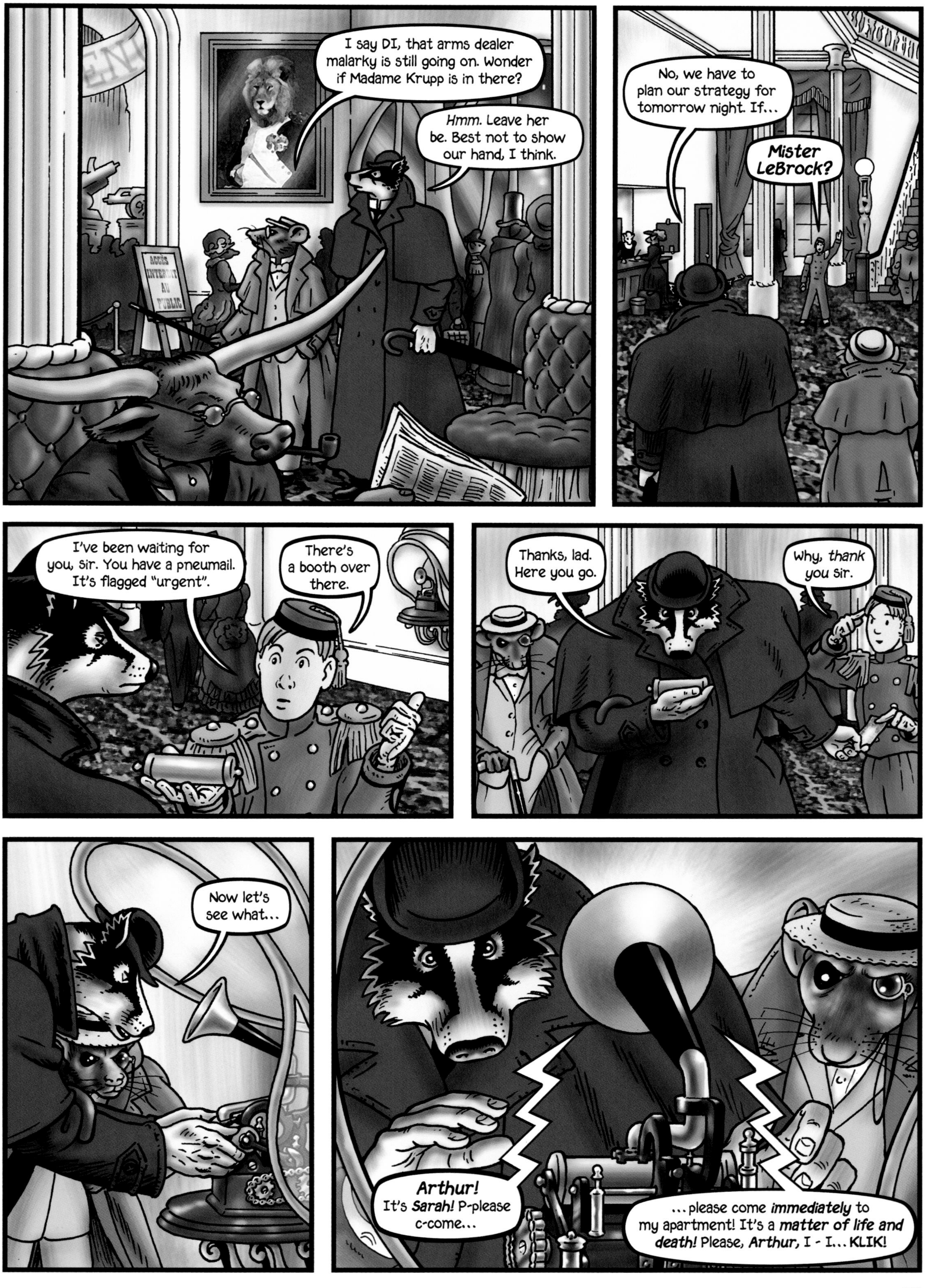

I say DI, that arms dealer malarky is still going on. Wonder if Madame Krupp is in there?
Hmm. Leave her be. Best not to show our hand, I think.
ACCÈS INTERDIT AU PUBLIC
No, we have to plan our strategy for tomorrow night. If...
Mister LeBrock?
I've been waiting for you, sir. You have a pneumail. It's flagged "urgent".
There's a booth over there.
Thanks, lad. Here you go.
Why, *thank* you sir.
Now let's see what...
Arthur! It's *Sarah!* P-please c-come...
...please come *immediately* to my apartment! It's a *matter of life and death!* Please, *Arthur,* I - I... KLIK!

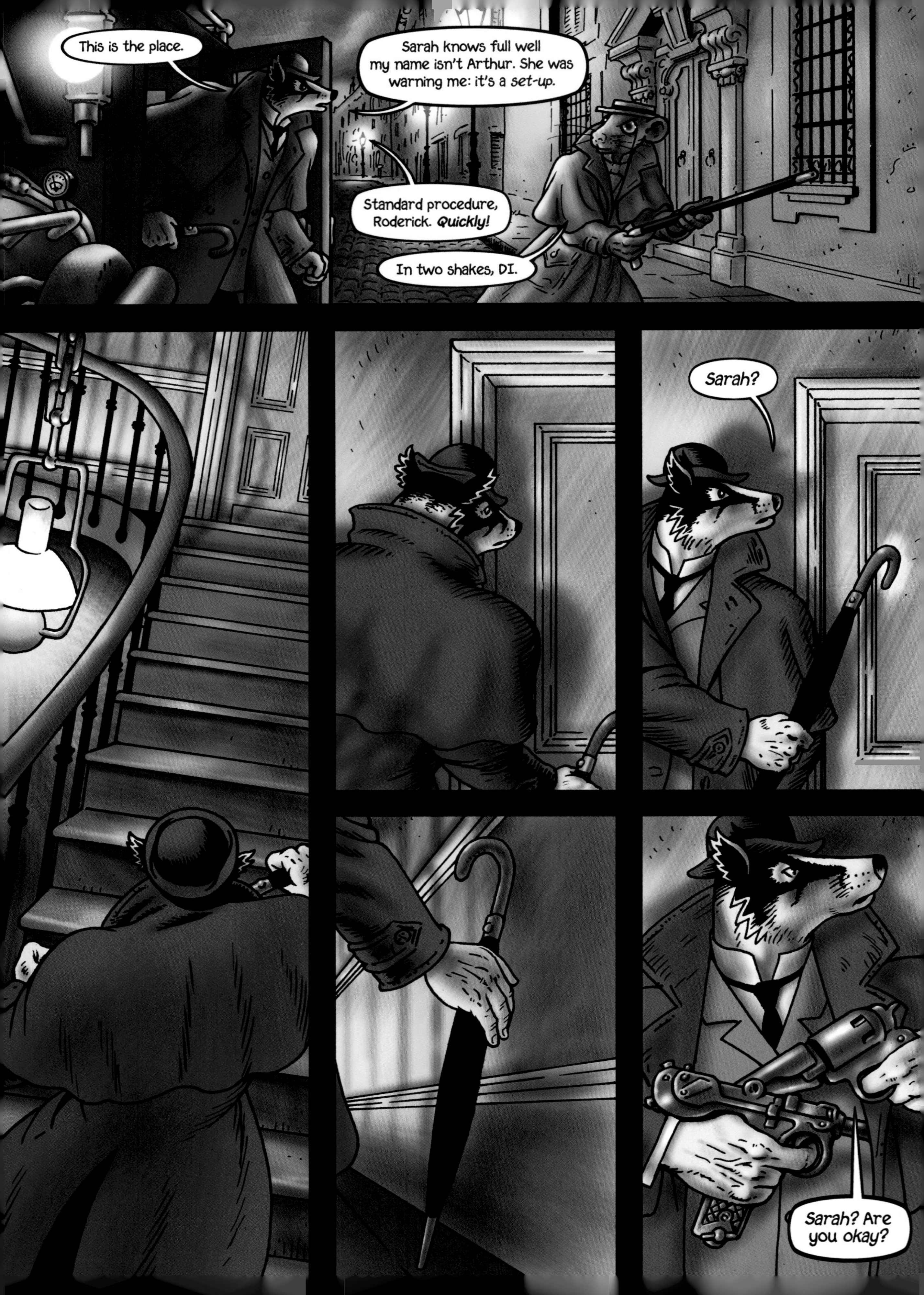

This is the place.
Sarah knows full well my name isn't Arthur. She was warning me: it's a *set-up*.
Standard procedure, Roderick. ***Quickly!***
In two shakes, DI.
Sarah?
Sarah? Are you okay?

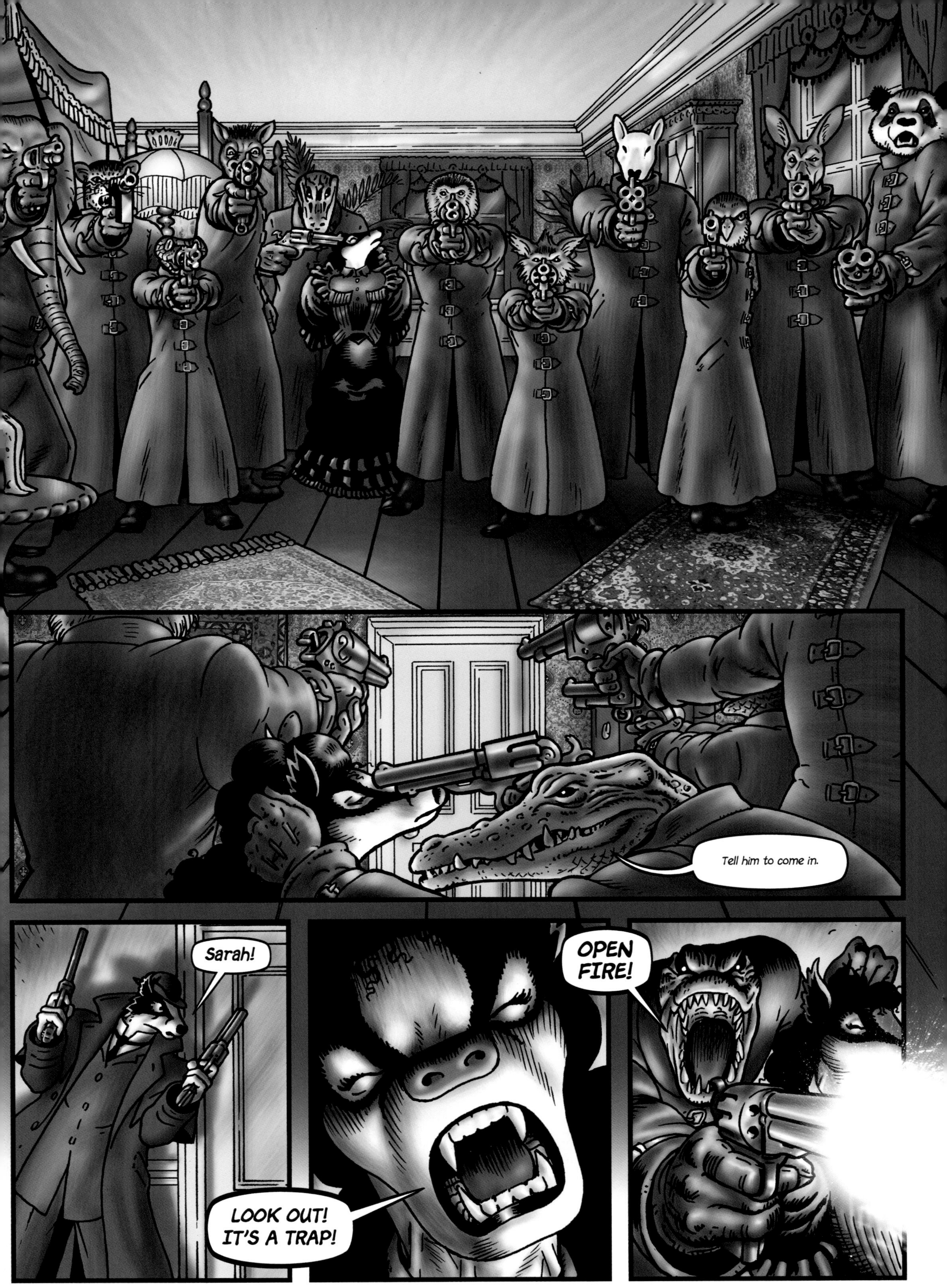
Tell him to come in.
Sarah!
LOOK OUT! IT'S A TRAP!
OPEN FIRE!

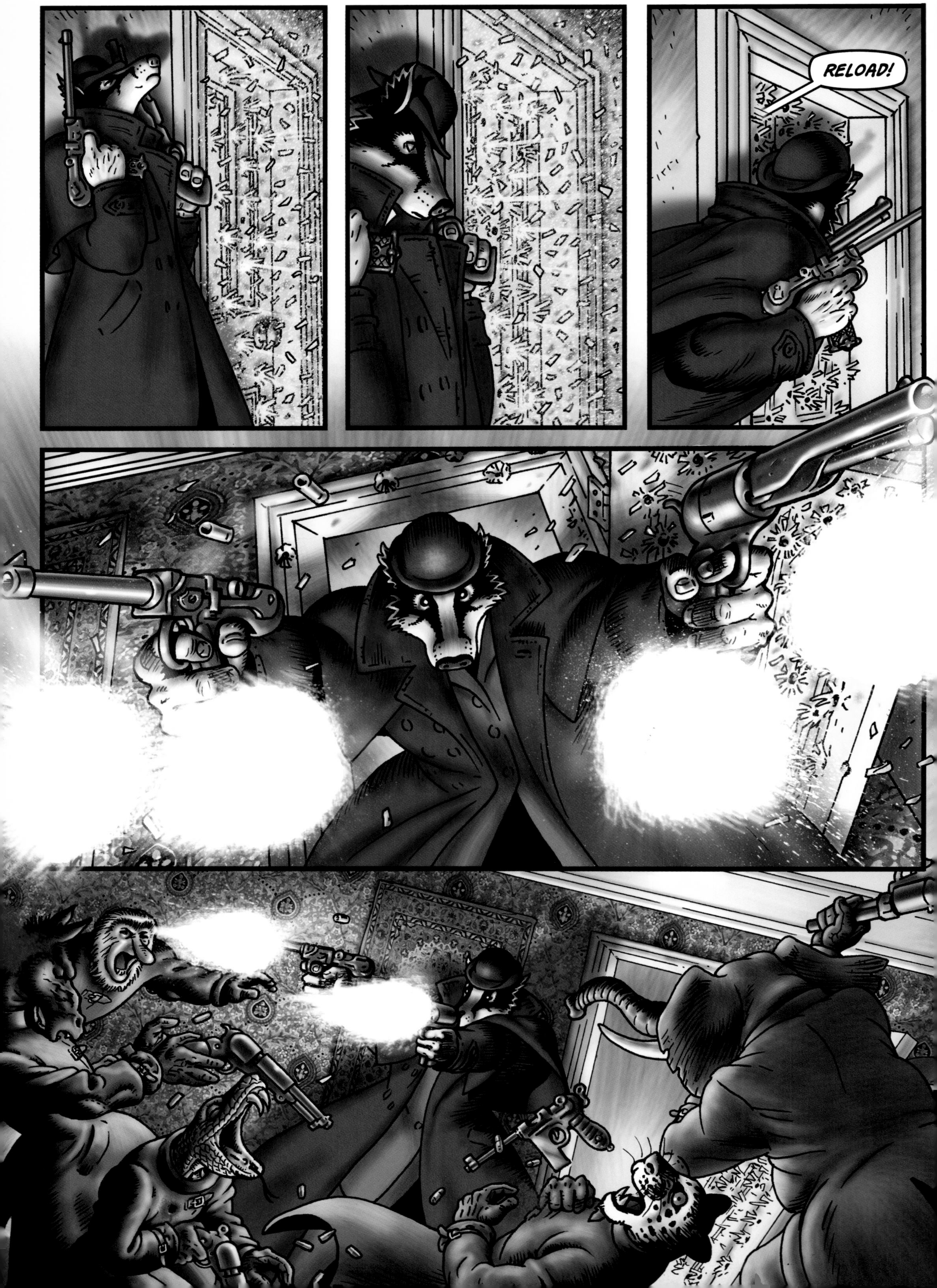
RELOAD!

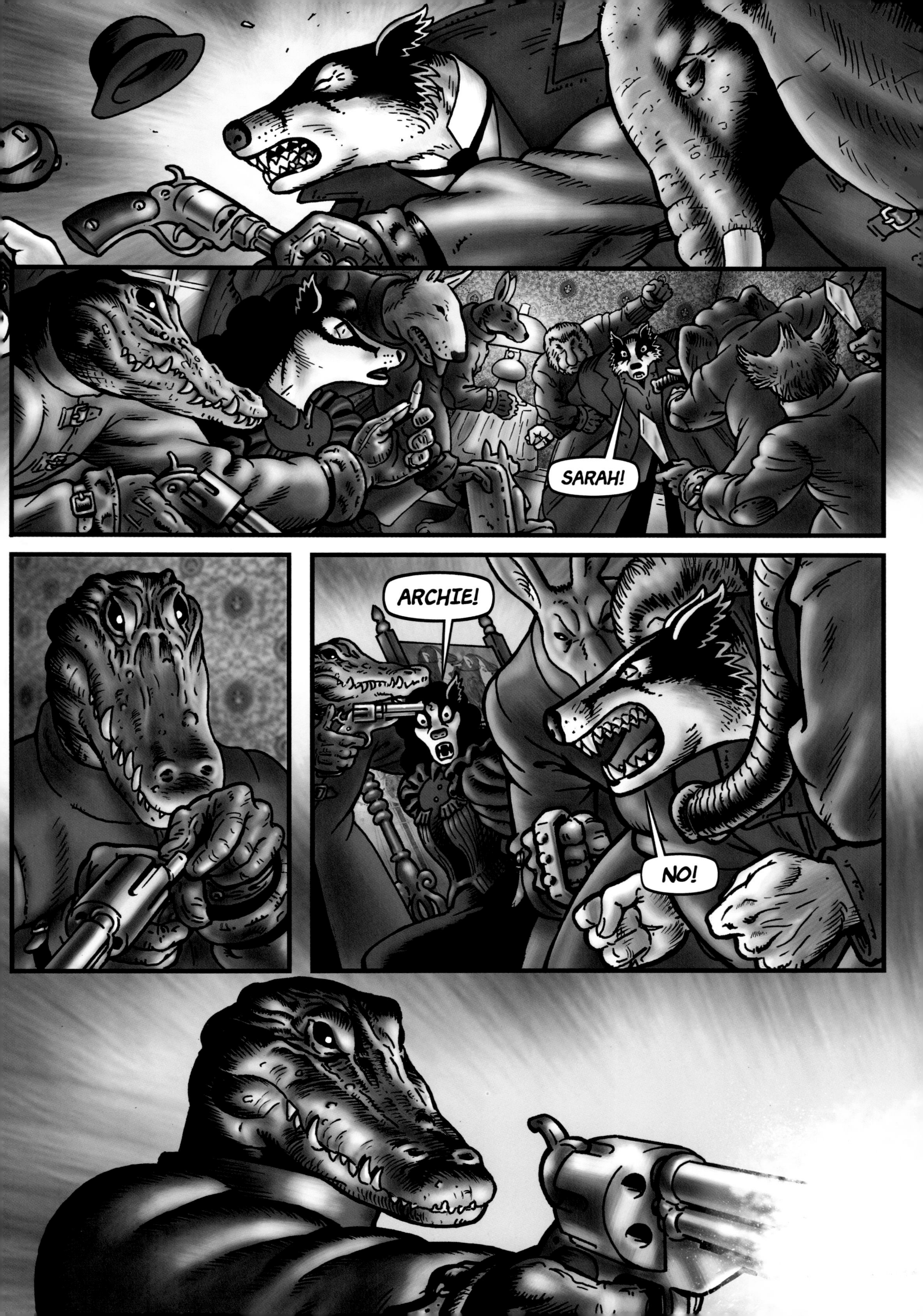
SARAH!
ARCHIE!
NO!

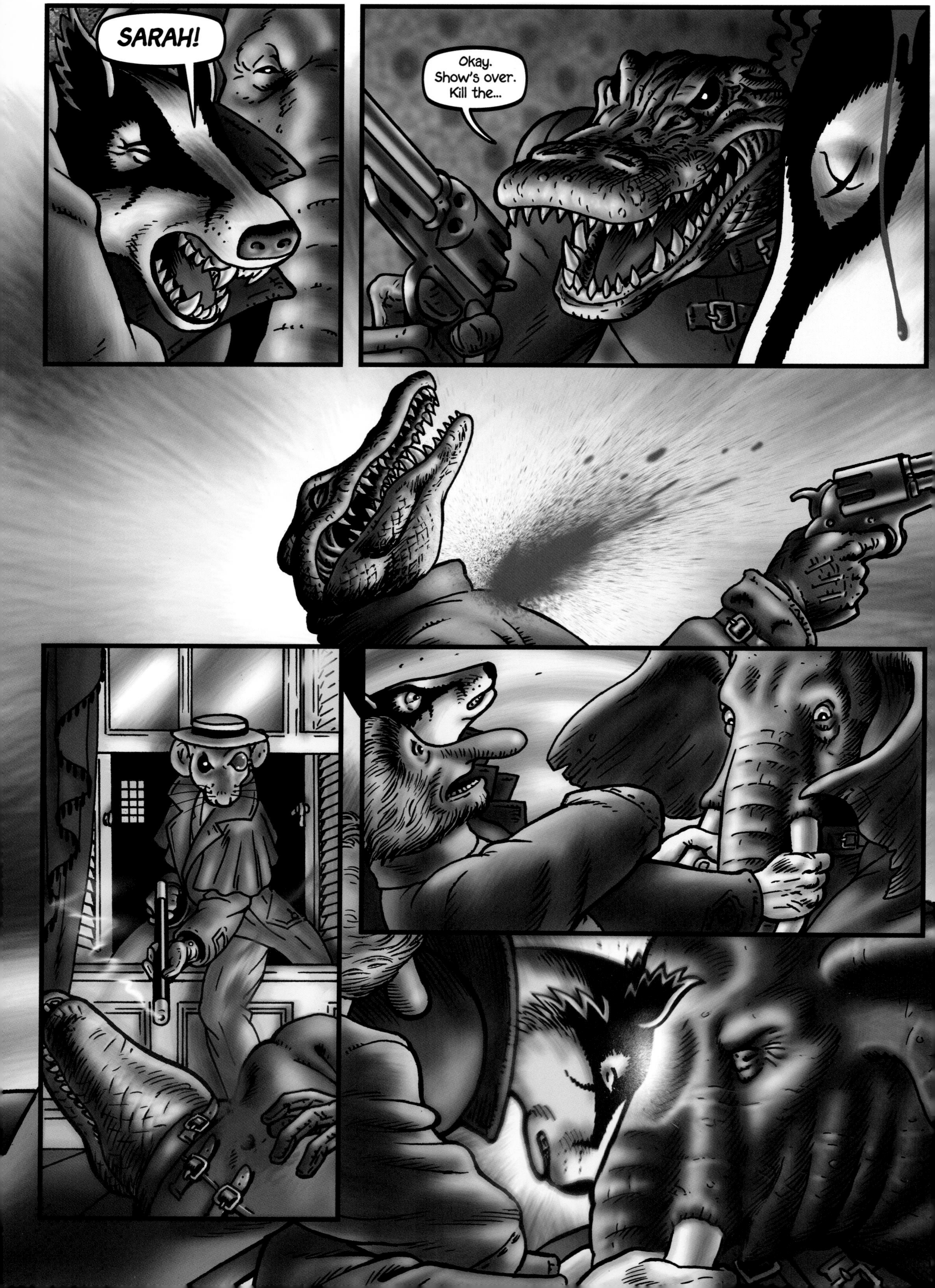
SARAH!
Okay. Show's over. Kill the...

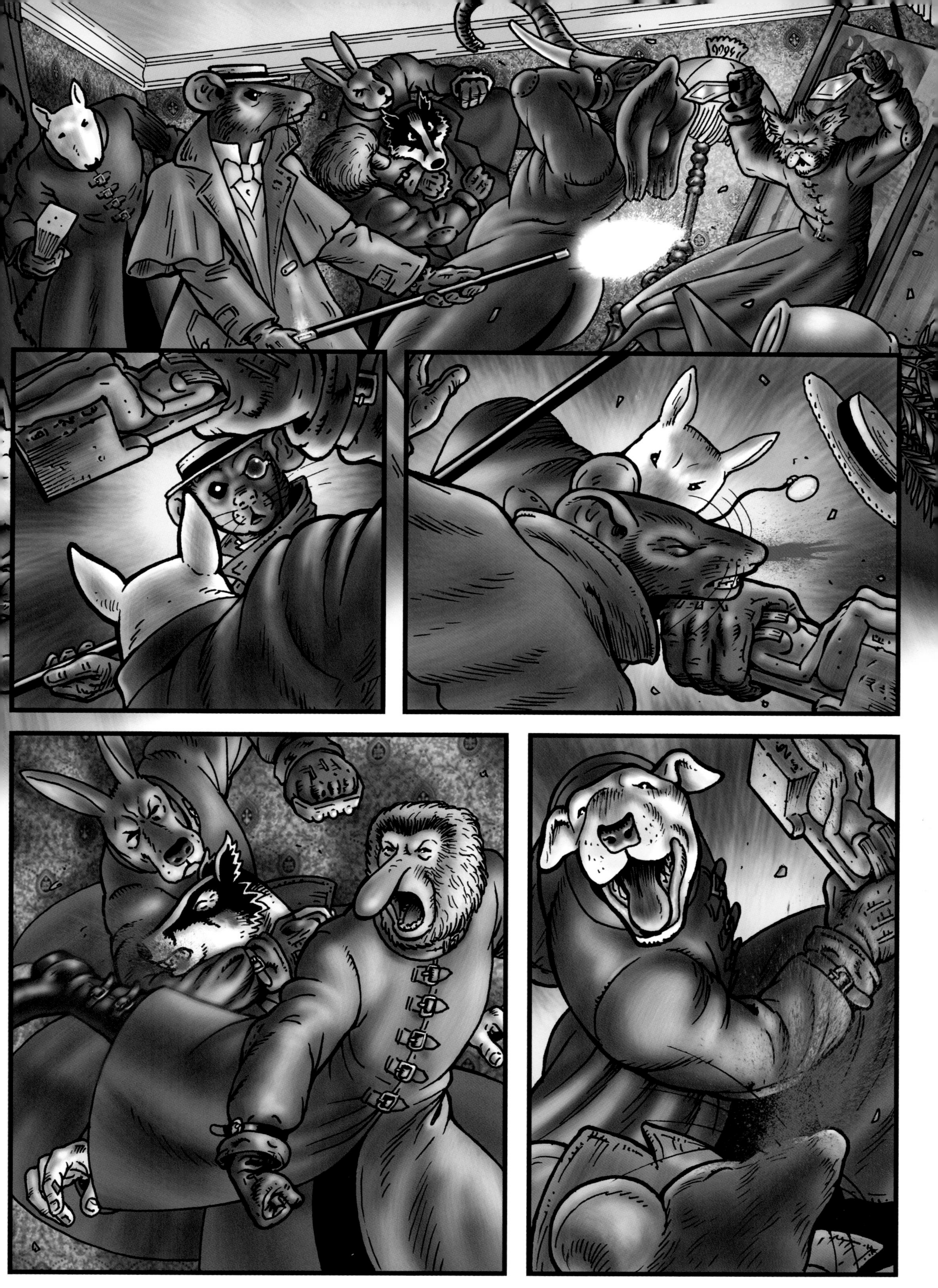

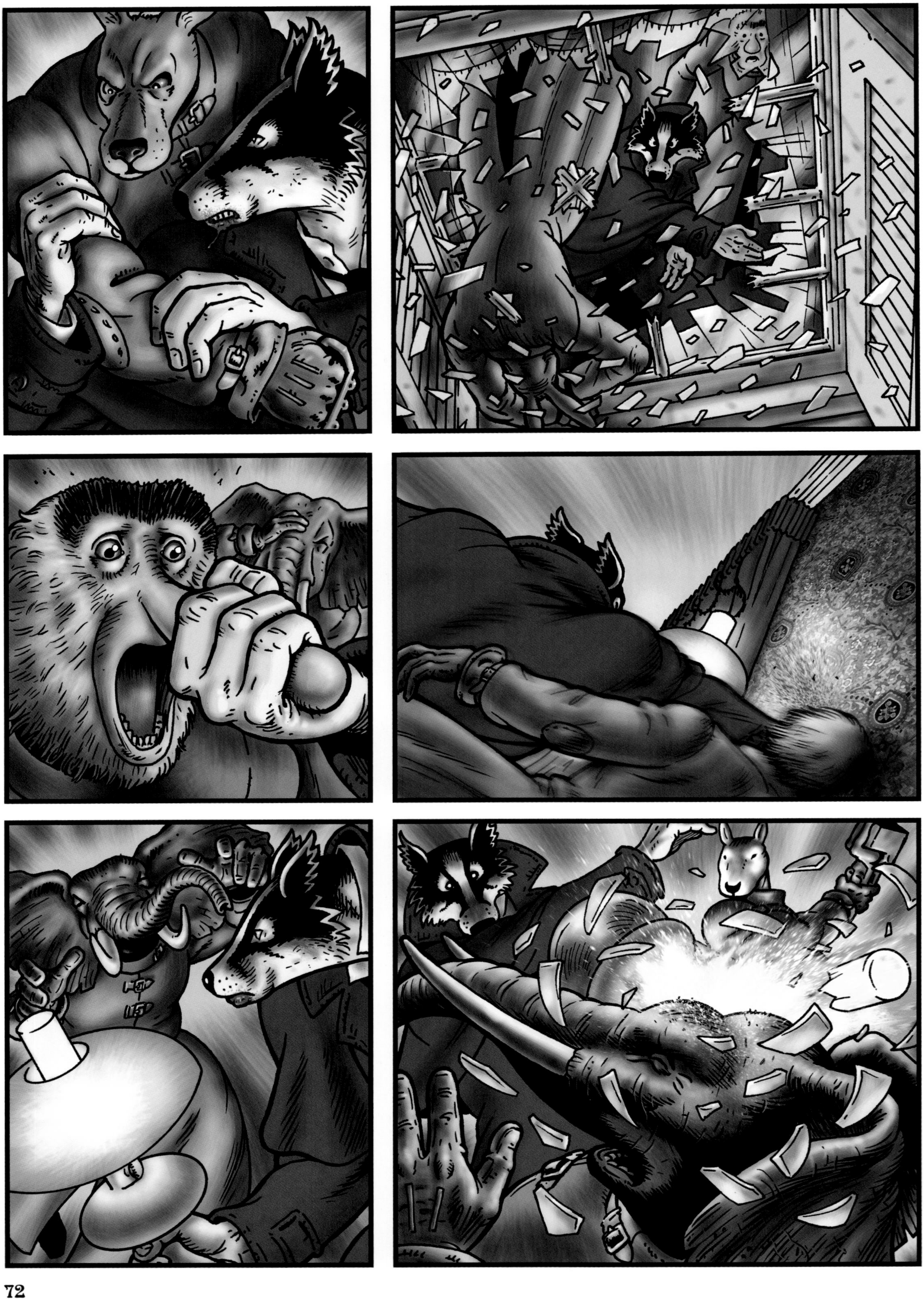

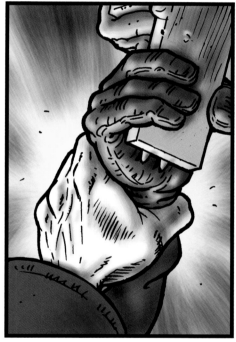

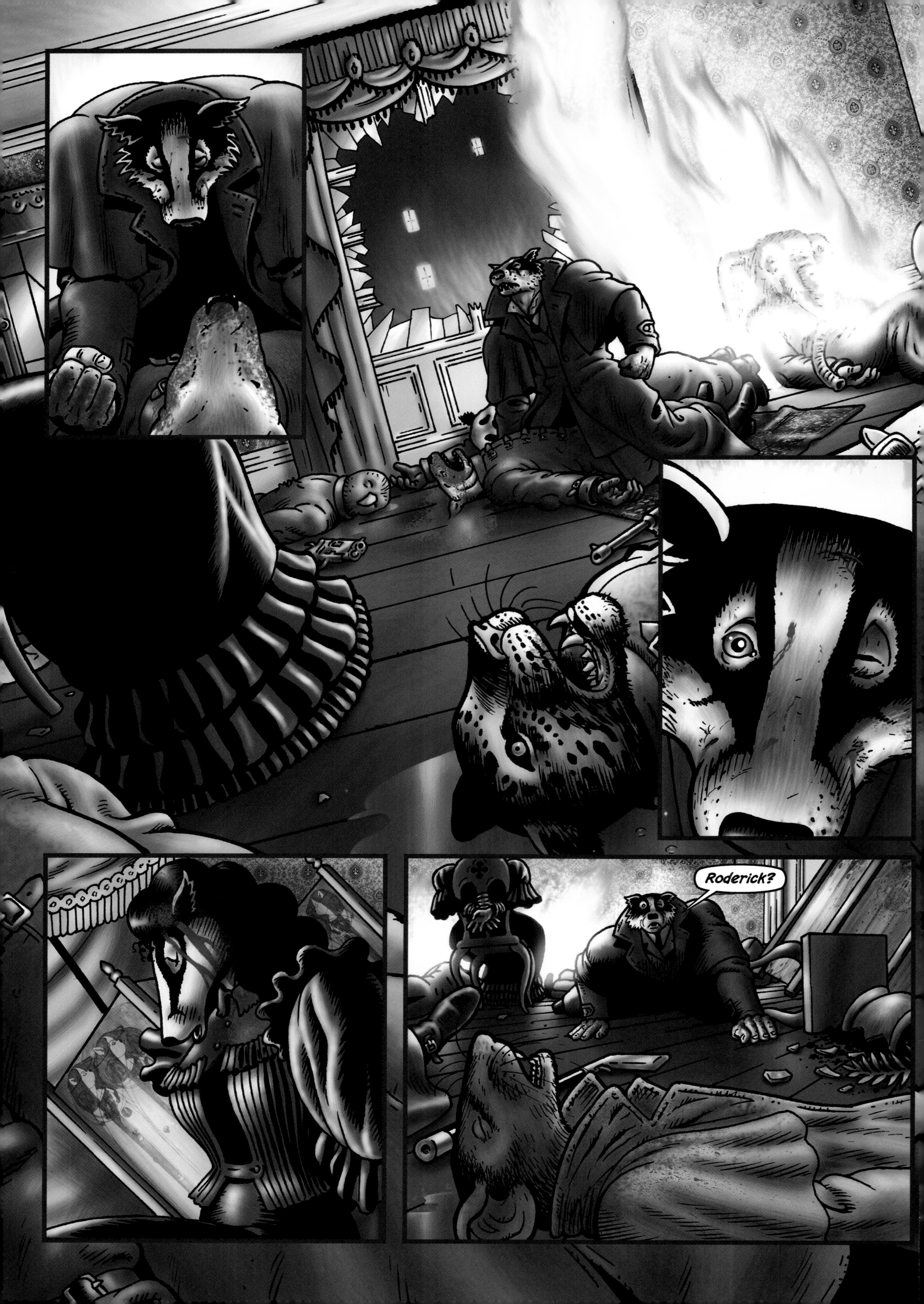
Roderick?

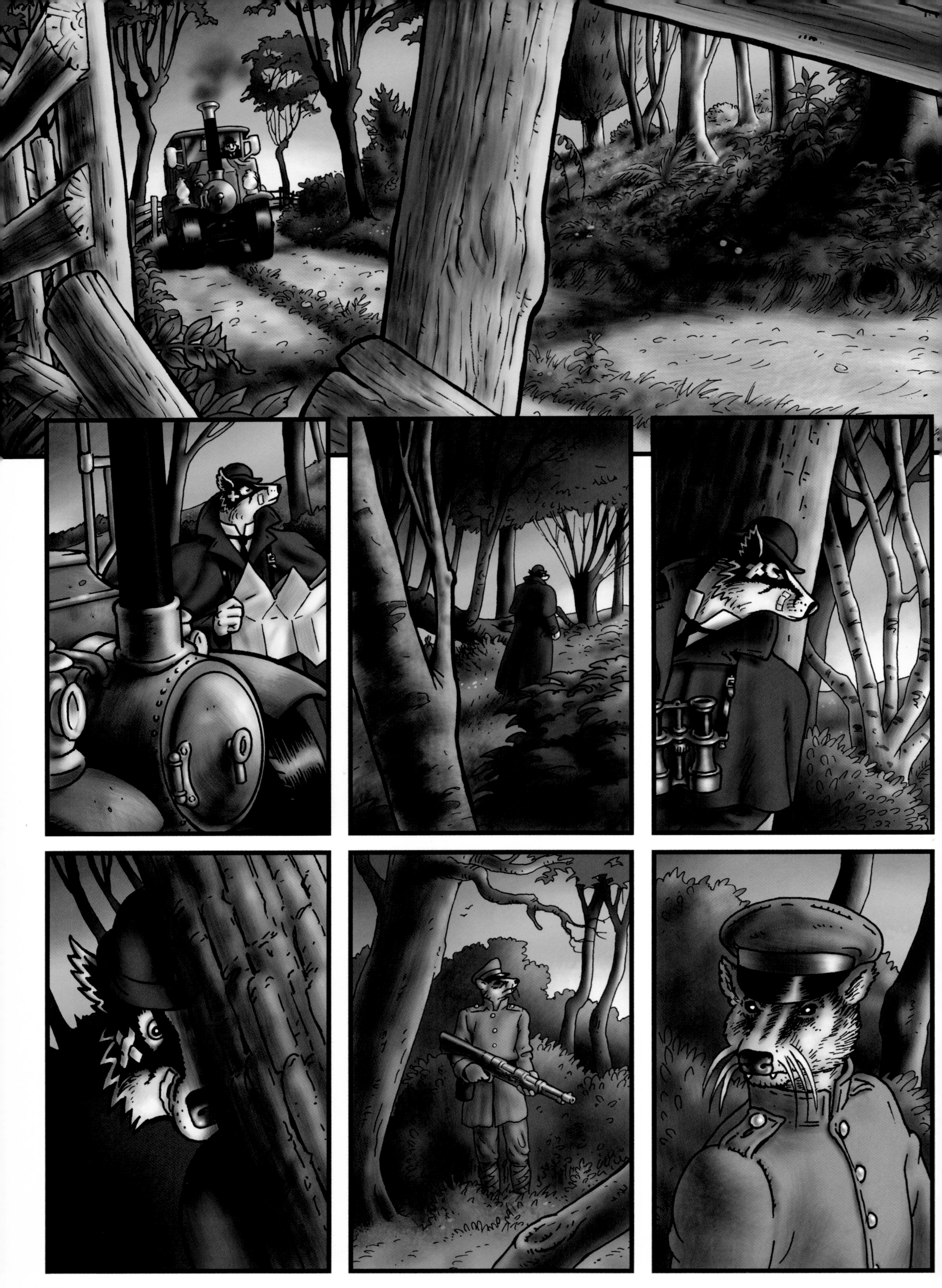

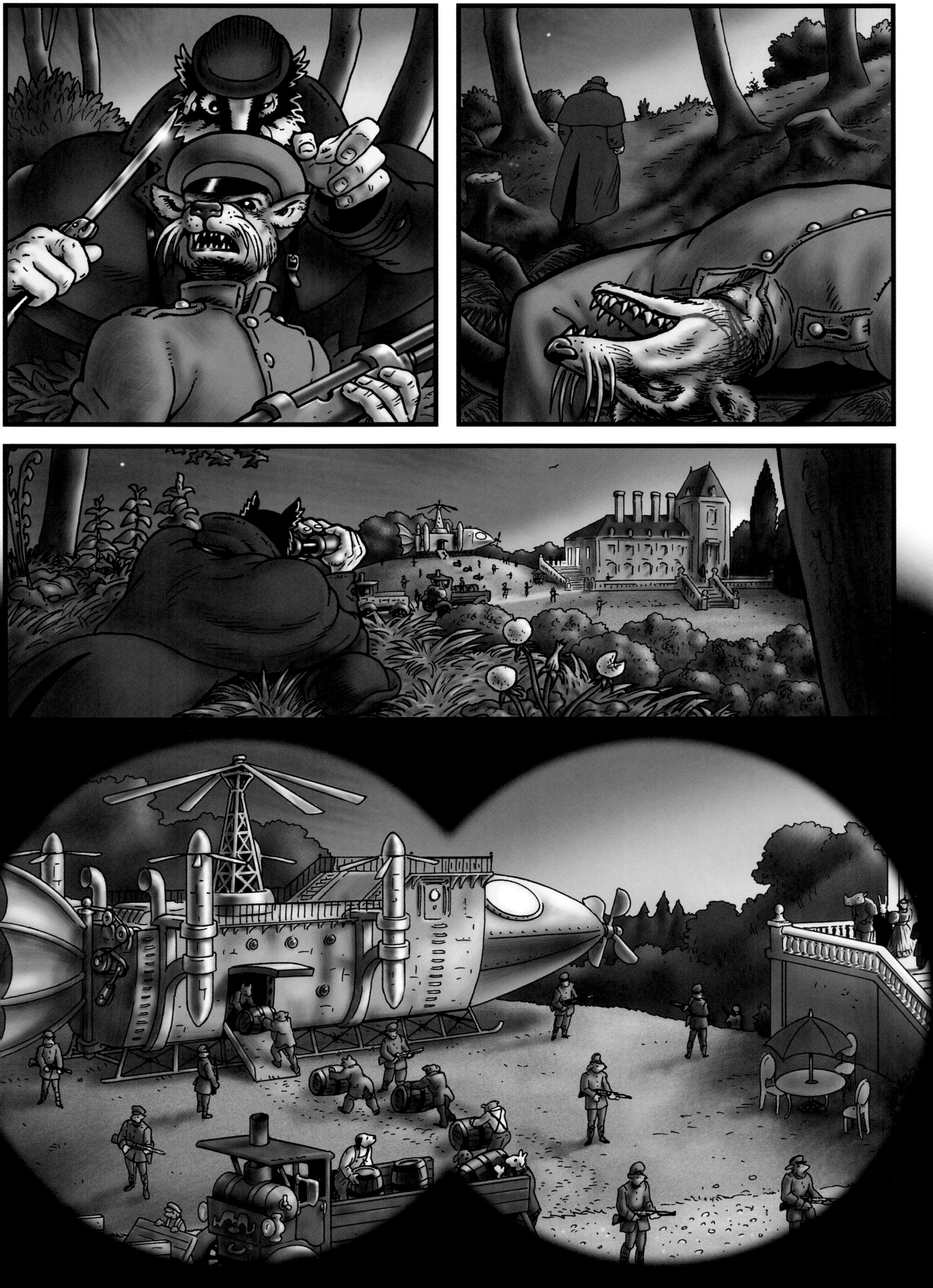

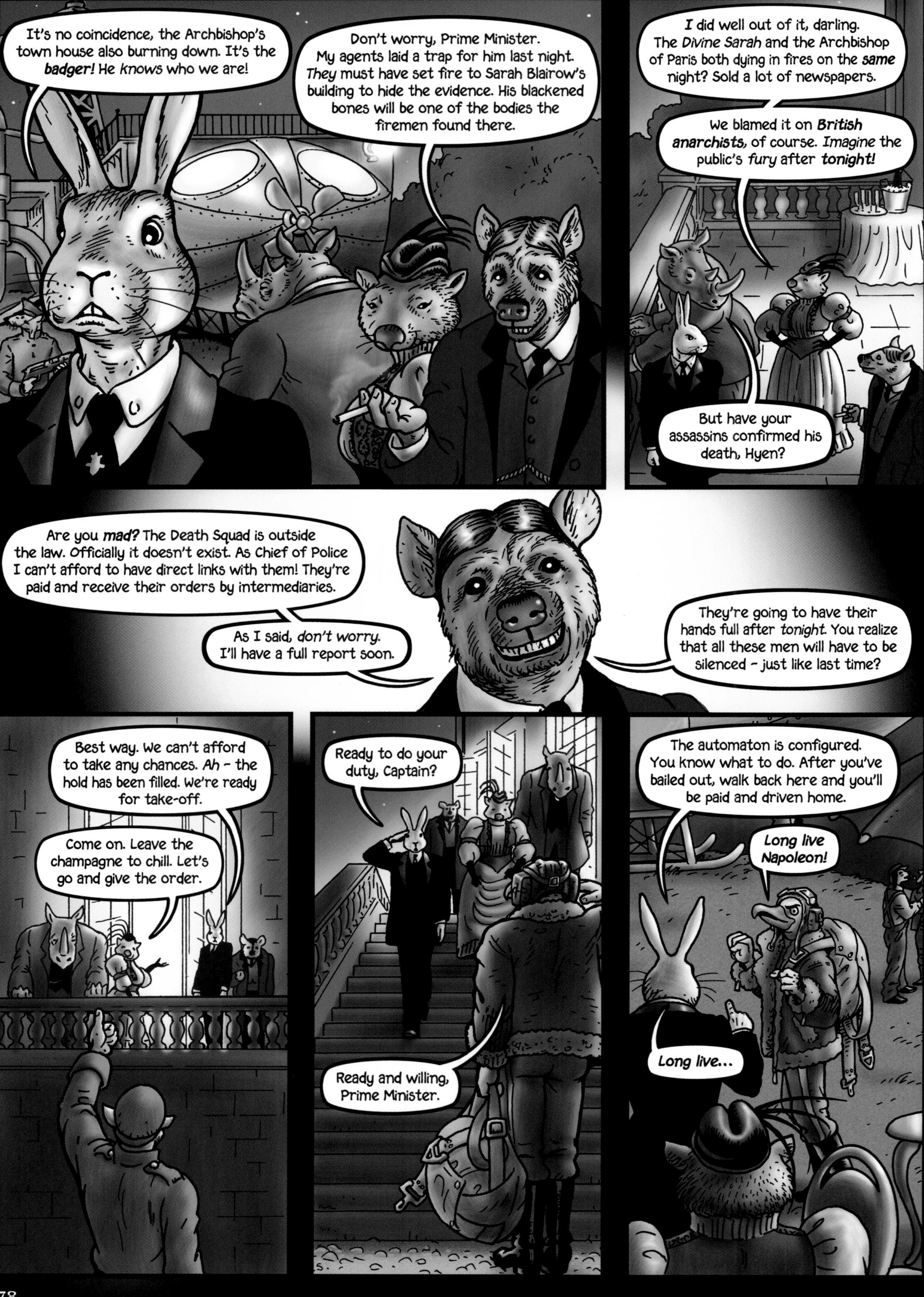

It's no coincidence, the Archbishop's town house also burning down. It's the *badger!* He *knows* who we are!
Don't worry, Prime Minister. My agents laid a trap for him last night. *They* must have set fire to Sarah Blairow's building to hide the evidence. His blackened bones will be one of the bodies the firemen found there.
I did well out of it, darling. The *Divine Sarah* and the Archbishop of Paris both dying in fires on the *same* night? Sold a lot of newspapers.
We blamed it on ***British anarchists***, of course. *Imagine* the public's *fury* after ***tonight!***
But have your assassins confirmed his death, Hyen?
Are you ***mad?*** The Death Squad is outside the law. Officially it doesn't exist. As Chief of Police I can't afford to have direct links with them! They're paid and receive their orders by intermediaries.
As I said, *don't worry.* I'll have a full report soon.
They're going to have their hands full after *tonight.* You realize that all these men will have to be silenced – just like last time?
Best way. We can't afford to take any chances. *Ah* – the hold has been filled. We're ready for take-off.
Come on. Leave the champagne to chill. Let's go and give the order.
Ready to do your duty, Captain?
Ready and willing, Prime Minister.
The automaton is configured. You know what to do. After you've bailed out, walk back here and you'll be paid and driven home.
Long live Napoleon!
Long live...

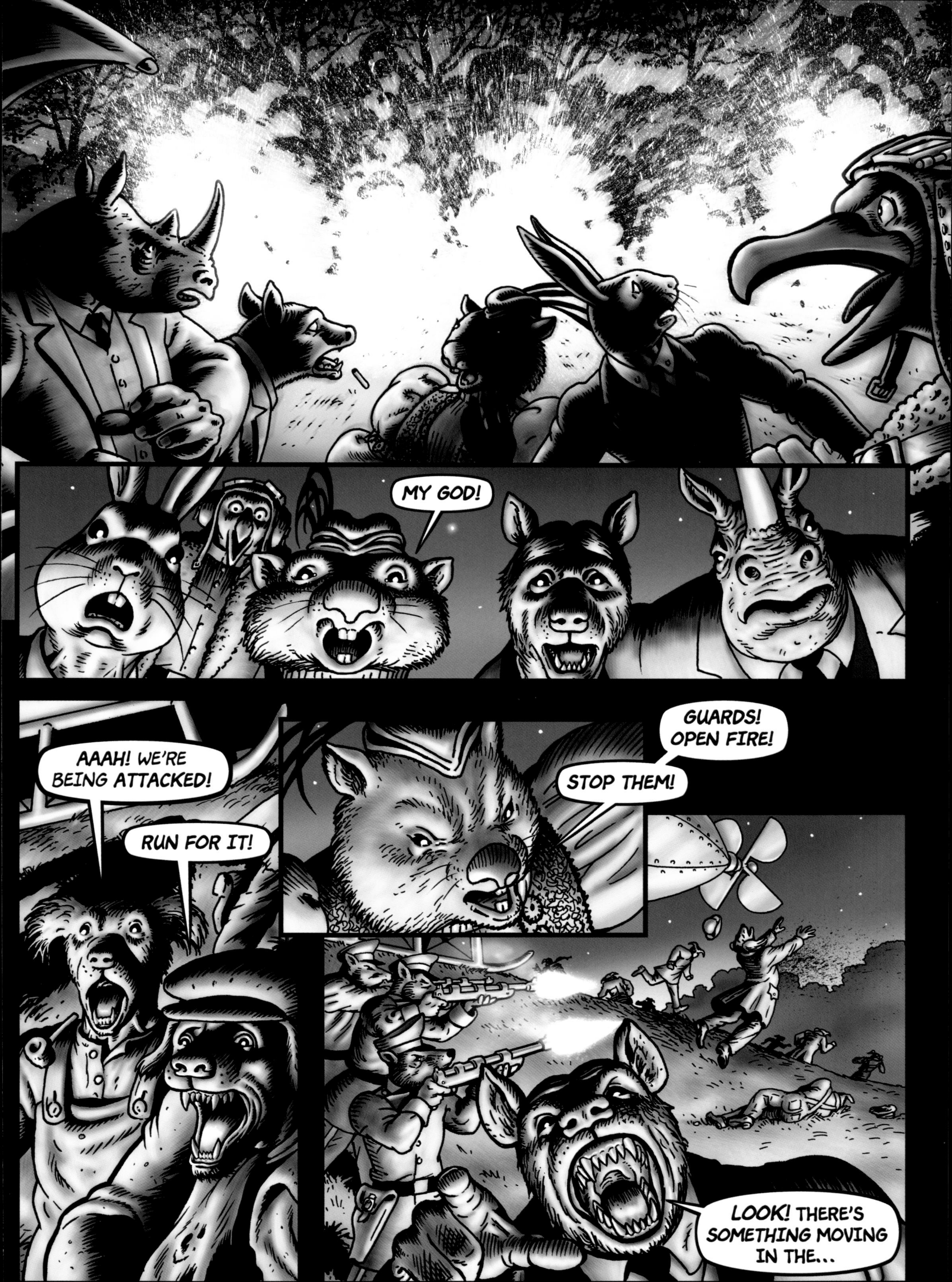
MY GOD!
AAAH! WE'RE BEING ATTACKED!
RUN FOR IT!
GUARDS! OPEN FIRE!
STOP THEM!
LOOK! THERE'S SOMETHING MOVING IN THE...

...trees.

IT'S... IT'S THE *BADGER!* KILL HIM! KILL HIM!

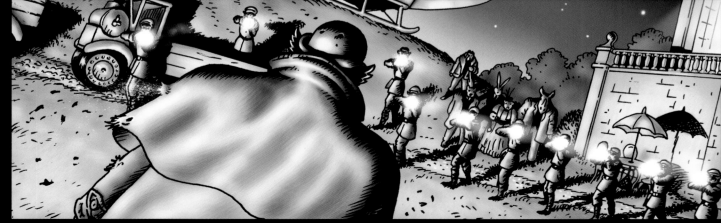

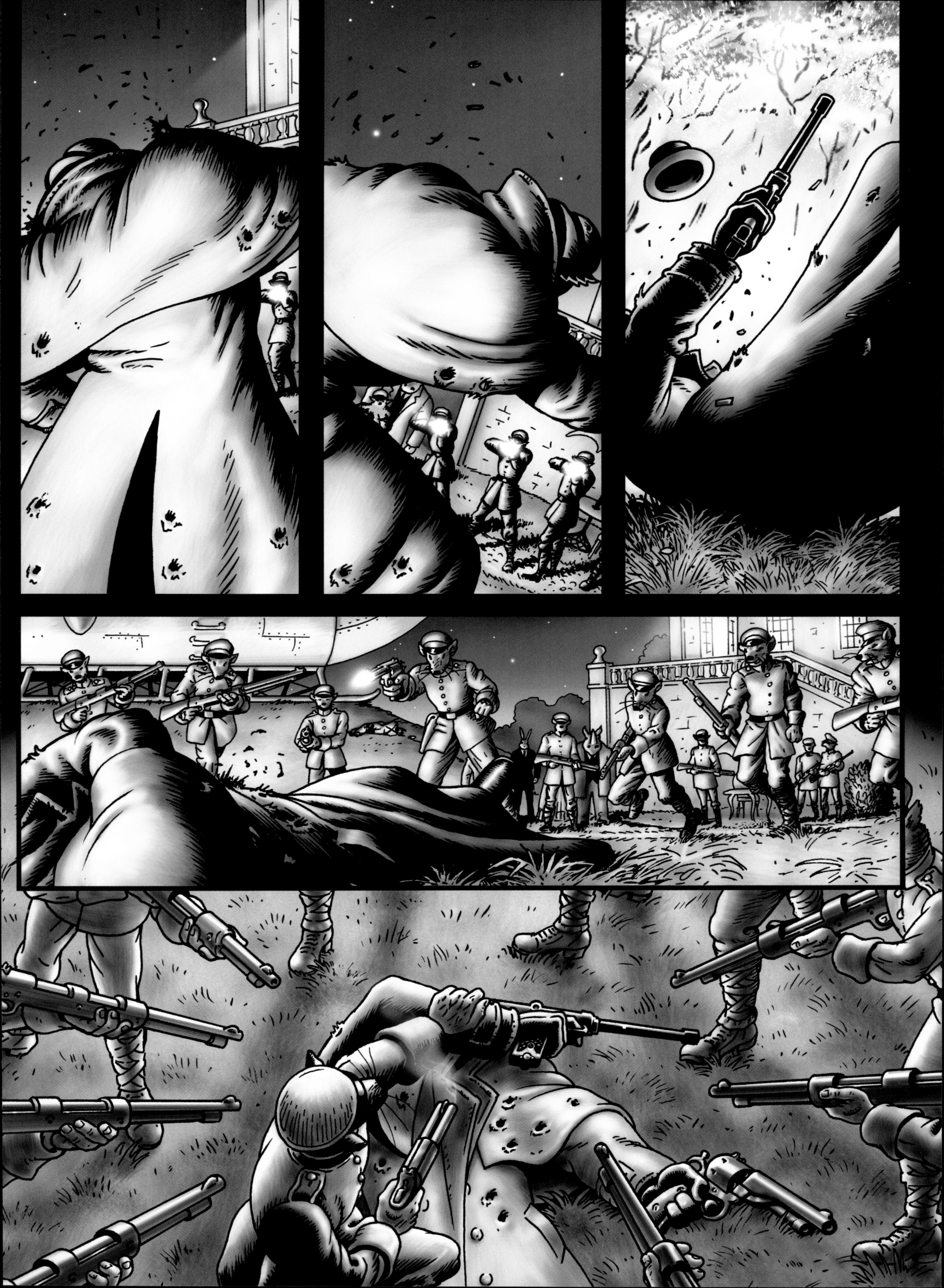

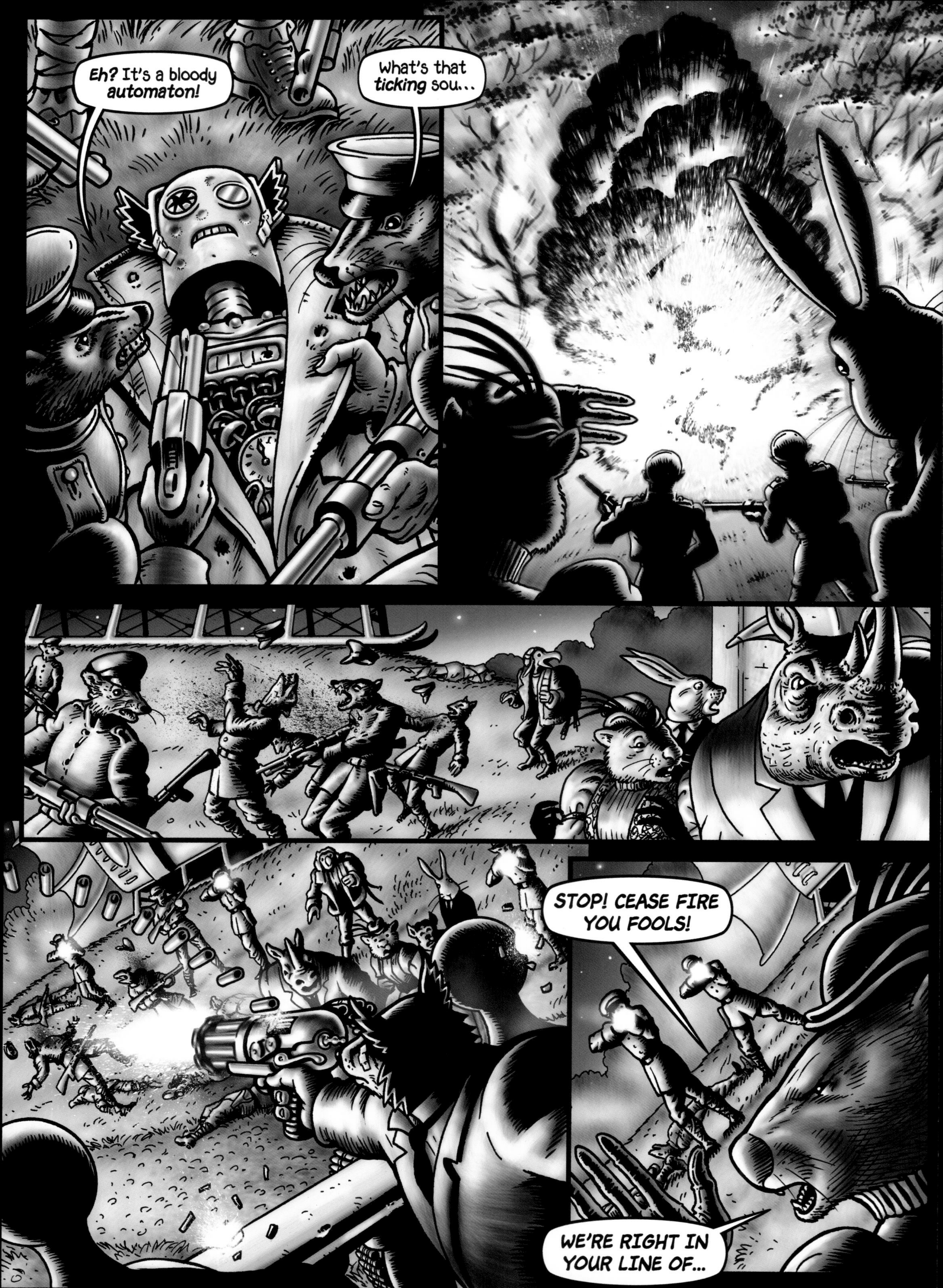
Eh? It's a bloody automaton!
What's that ticking sou…
STOP! CEASE FIRE YOU FOOLS!
WE'RE RIGHT IN YOUR LINE OF…

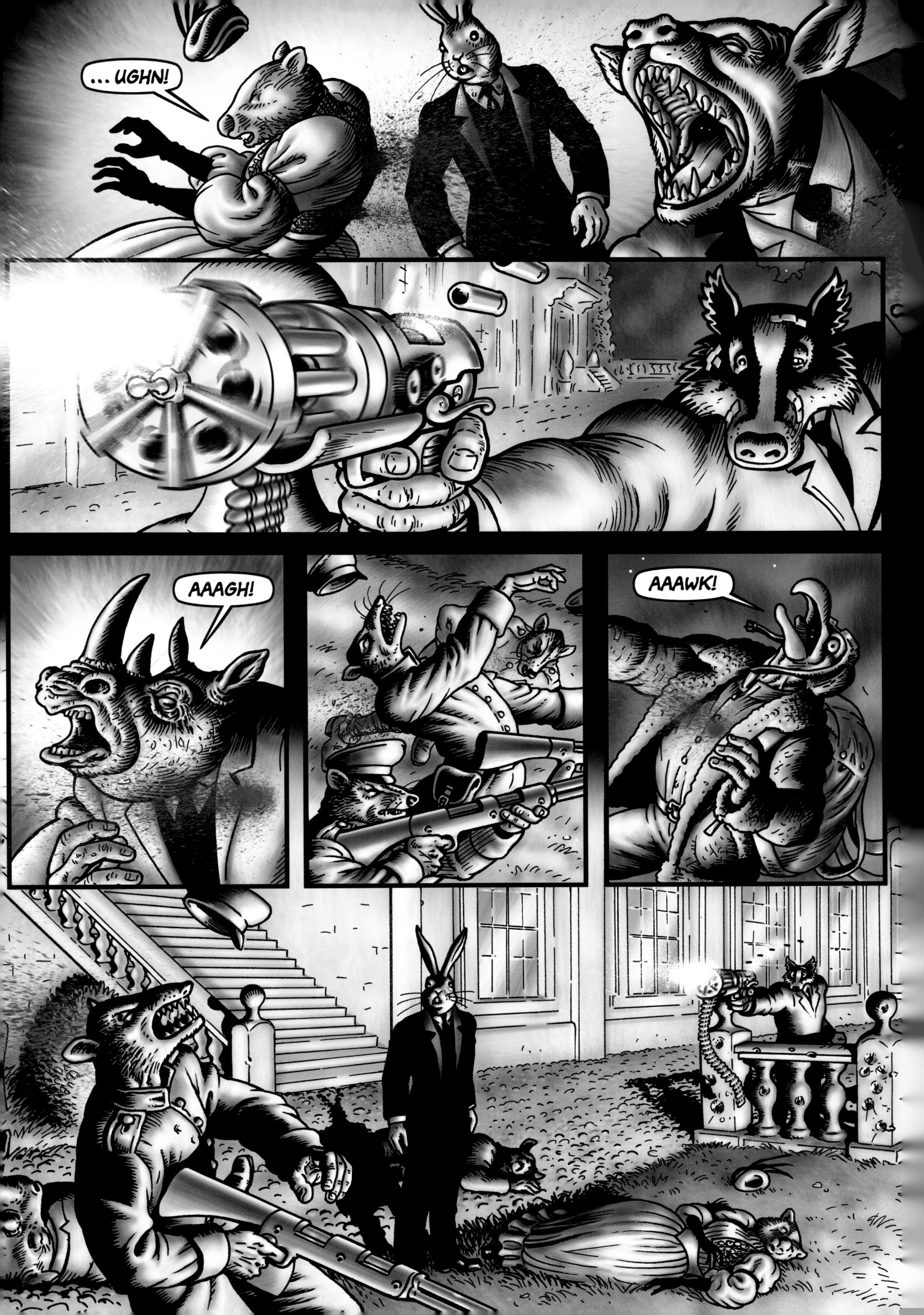
...UGHN!
AAAGH!
AAAWK!

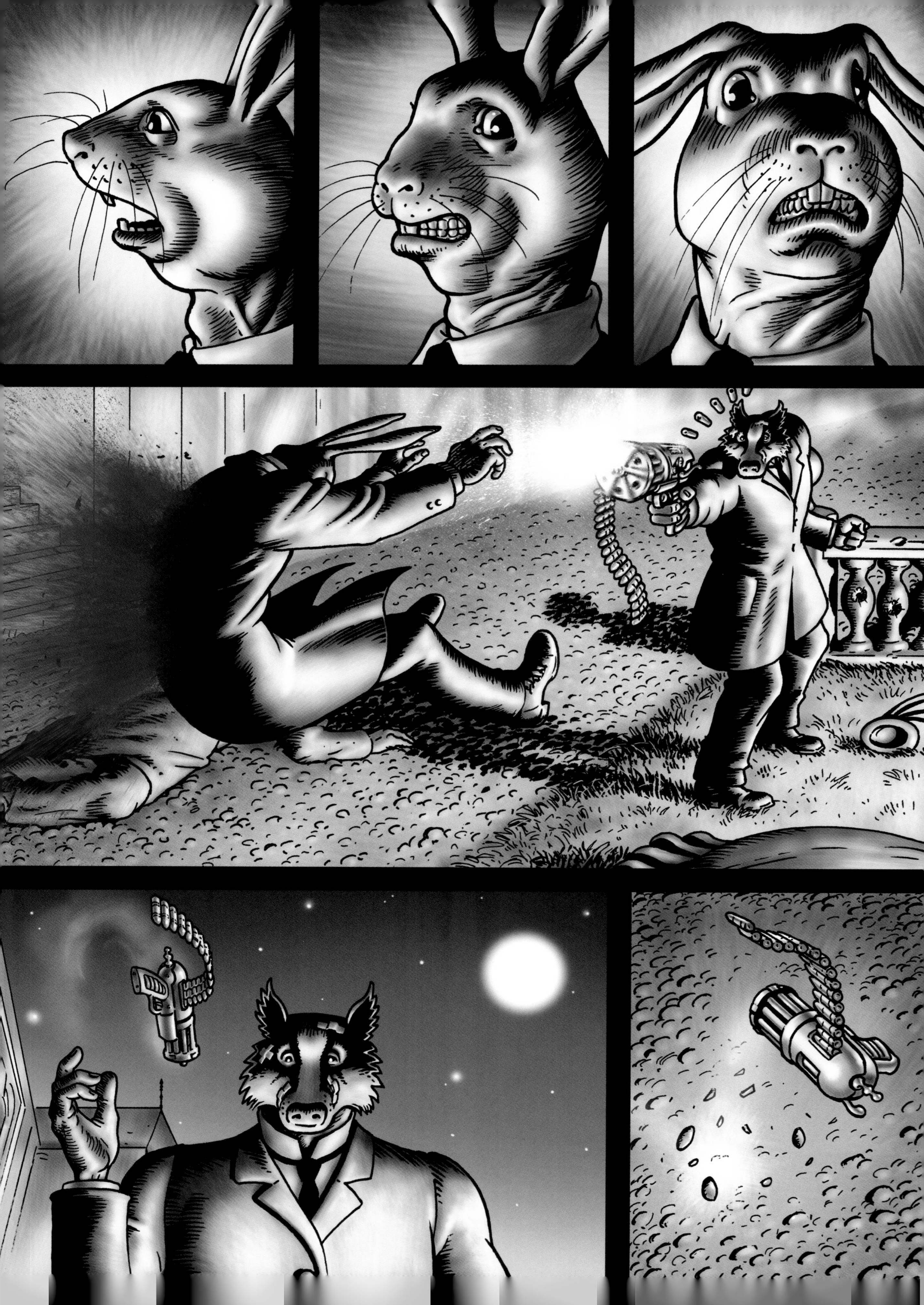

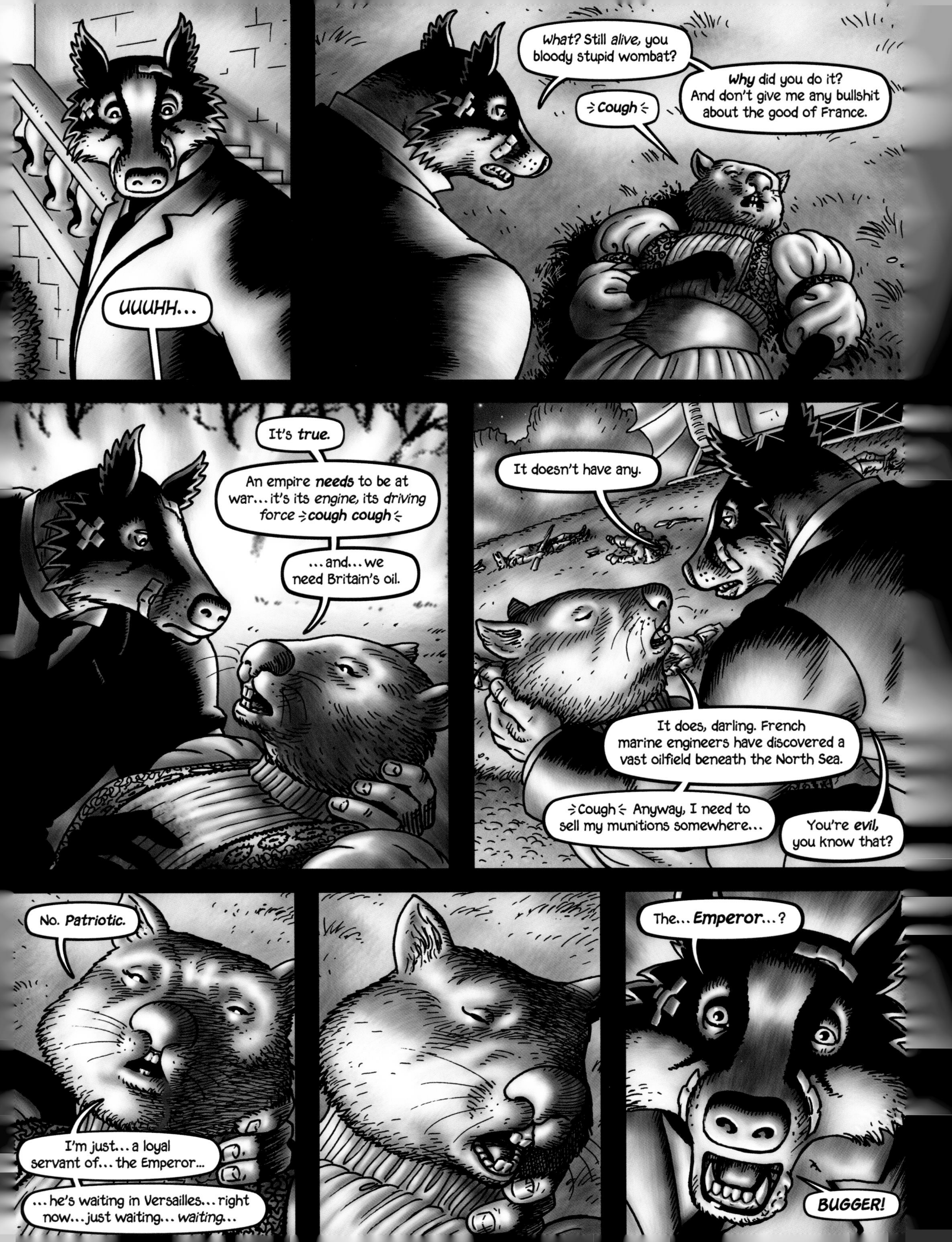
UUUHH...
What? Still *alive*, you bloody stupid wombat?
Cough
Why did you do it? And don't give me any bullshit about the good of France.
It's *true.*
An empire **needs** to be at war... it's its *engine*, its *driving force* **cough cough**
...and... we need Britain's oil.
It doesn't have any.
It does, darling. French marine engineers have discovered a vast oilfield beneath the North Sea.
Cough Anyway, I need to sell my munitions somewhere...
You're *evil*, you know that?
No. *Patriotic.*
I'm just... a loyal servant of... the Emperor...
...he's waiting in Versailles... right now... just waiting... *waiting*...
The... **Emperor**...?
BUGGER!

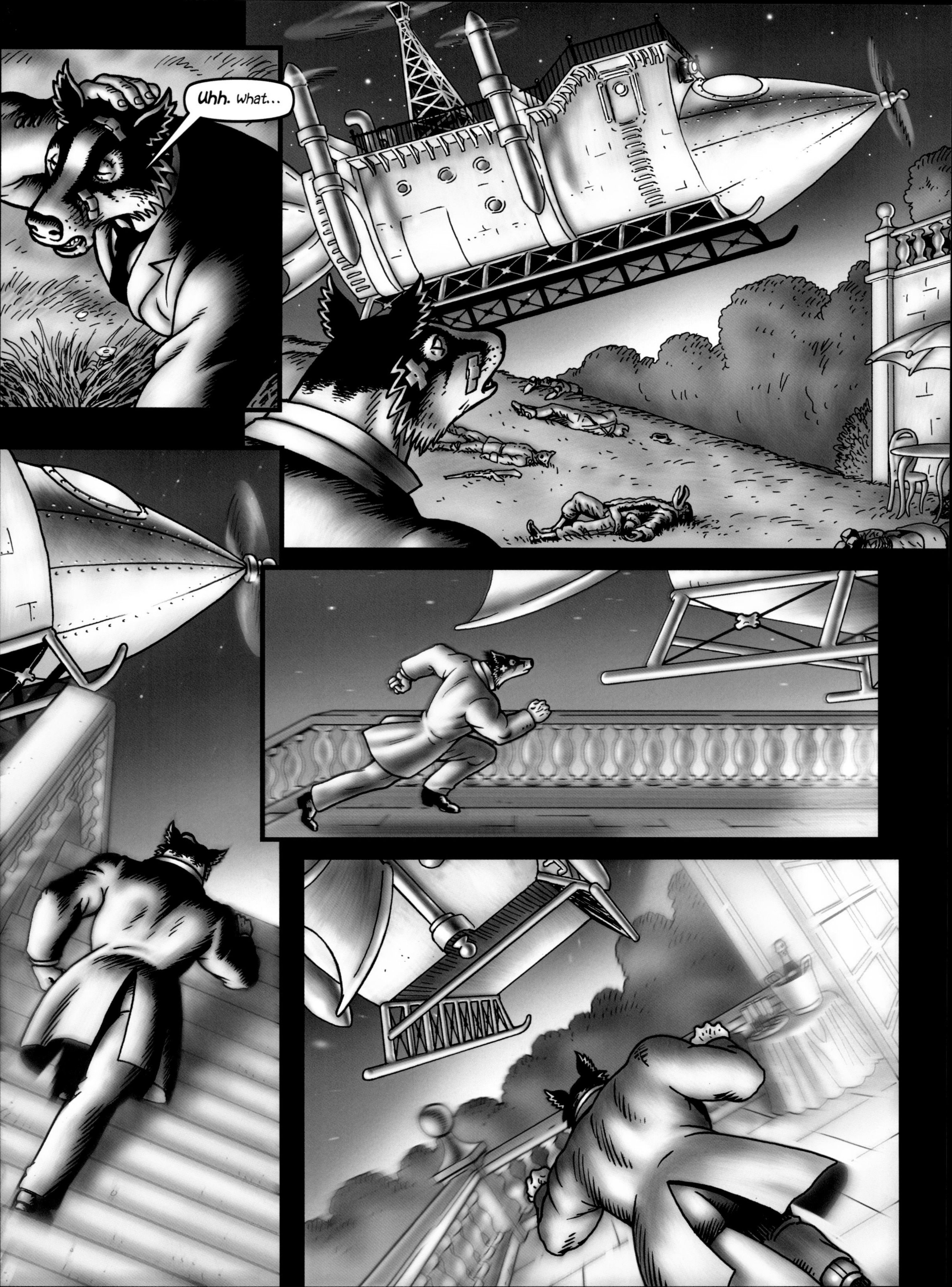
Uhh. What...

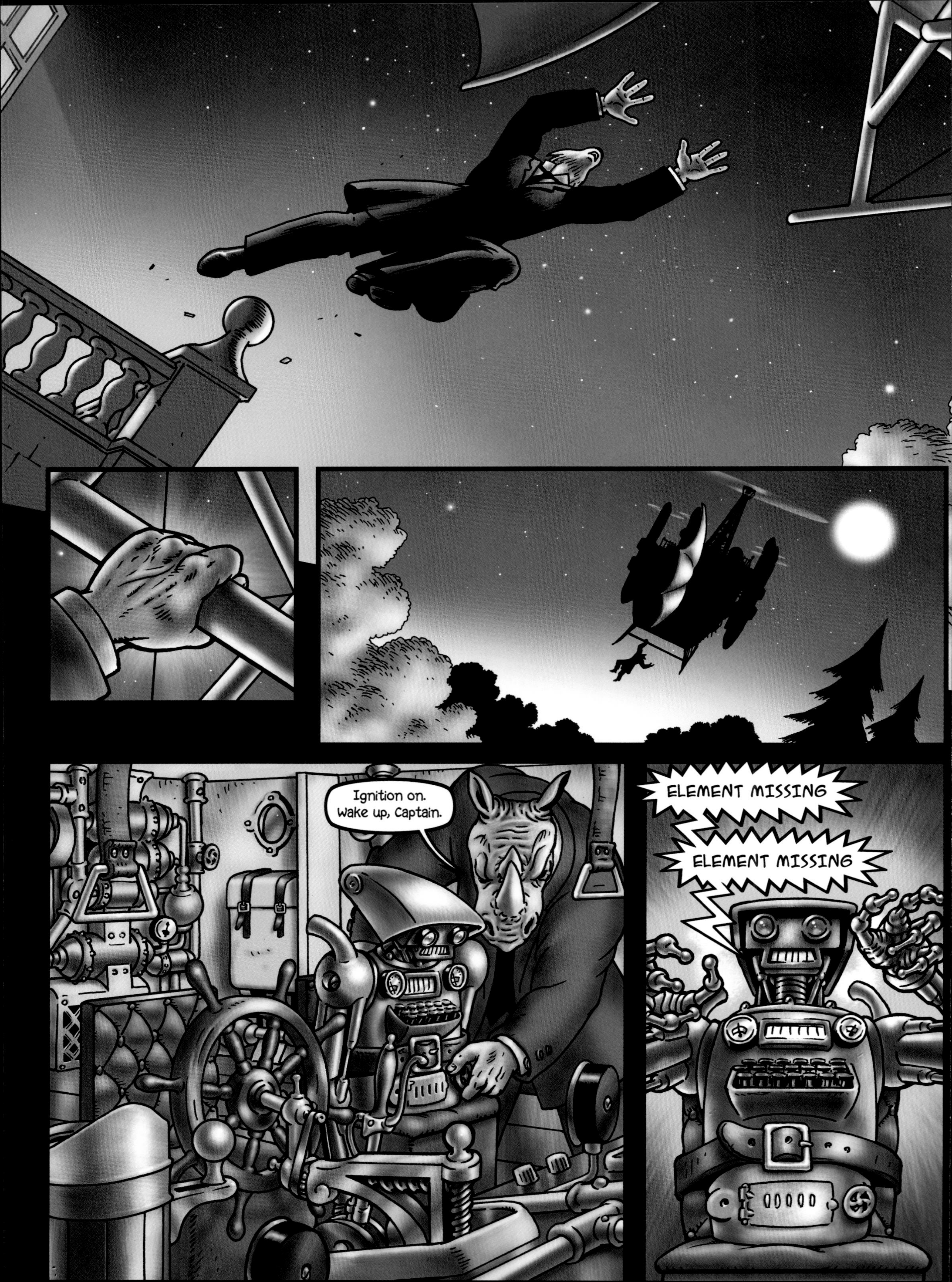
Ignition on.
Wake up, Captain.
ELEMENT MISSING
ELEMENT MISSING

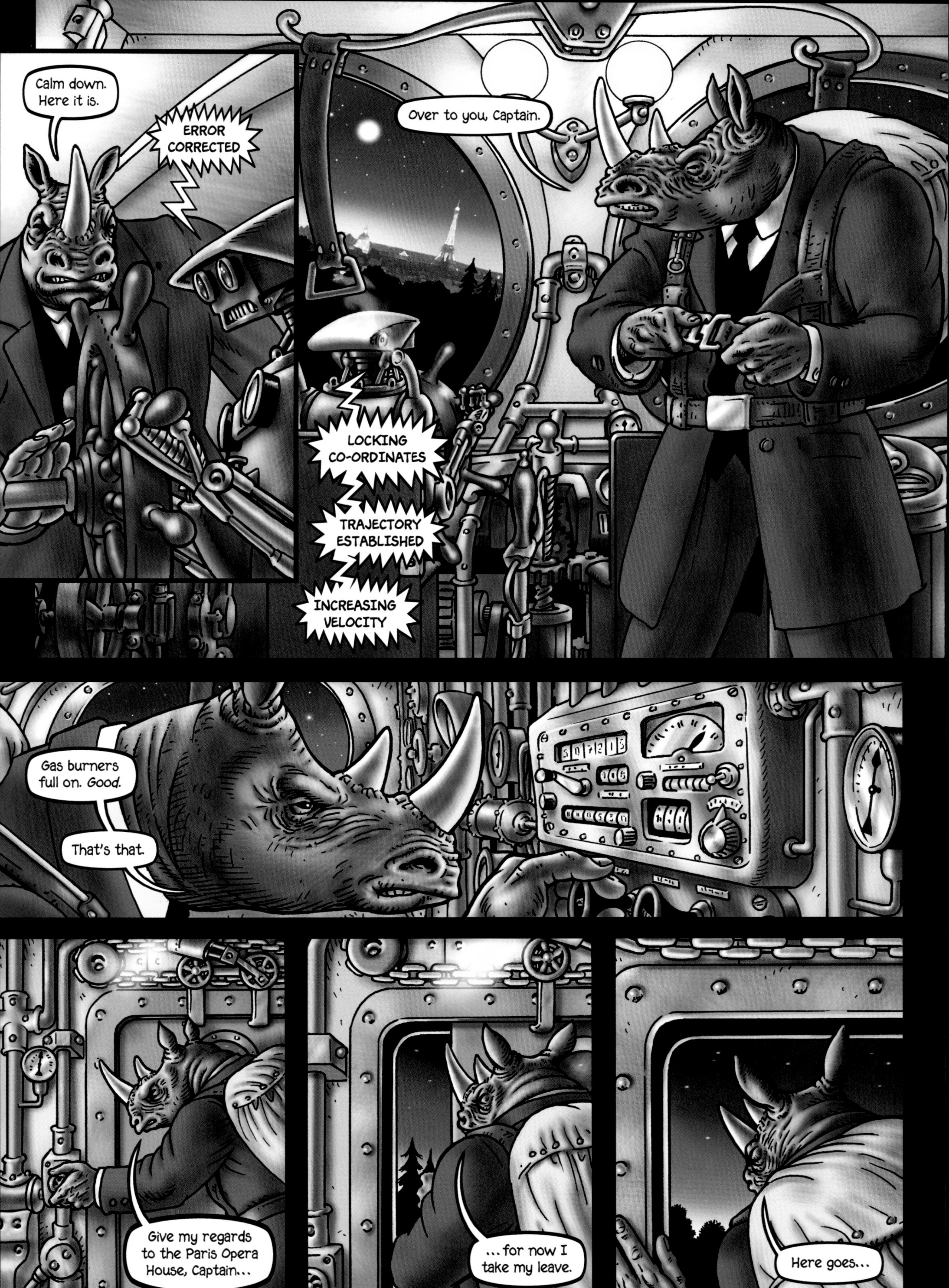
Calm down. Here it is.
ERROR CORRECTED
Over to you, Captain.
LOCKING CO-ORDINATES
TRAJECTORY ESTABLISHED
INCREASING VELOCITY
Gas burners full on. *Good.*
That's that.
Give my regards to the Paris Opera House, Captain...
...for now I take my leave.
Here goes...

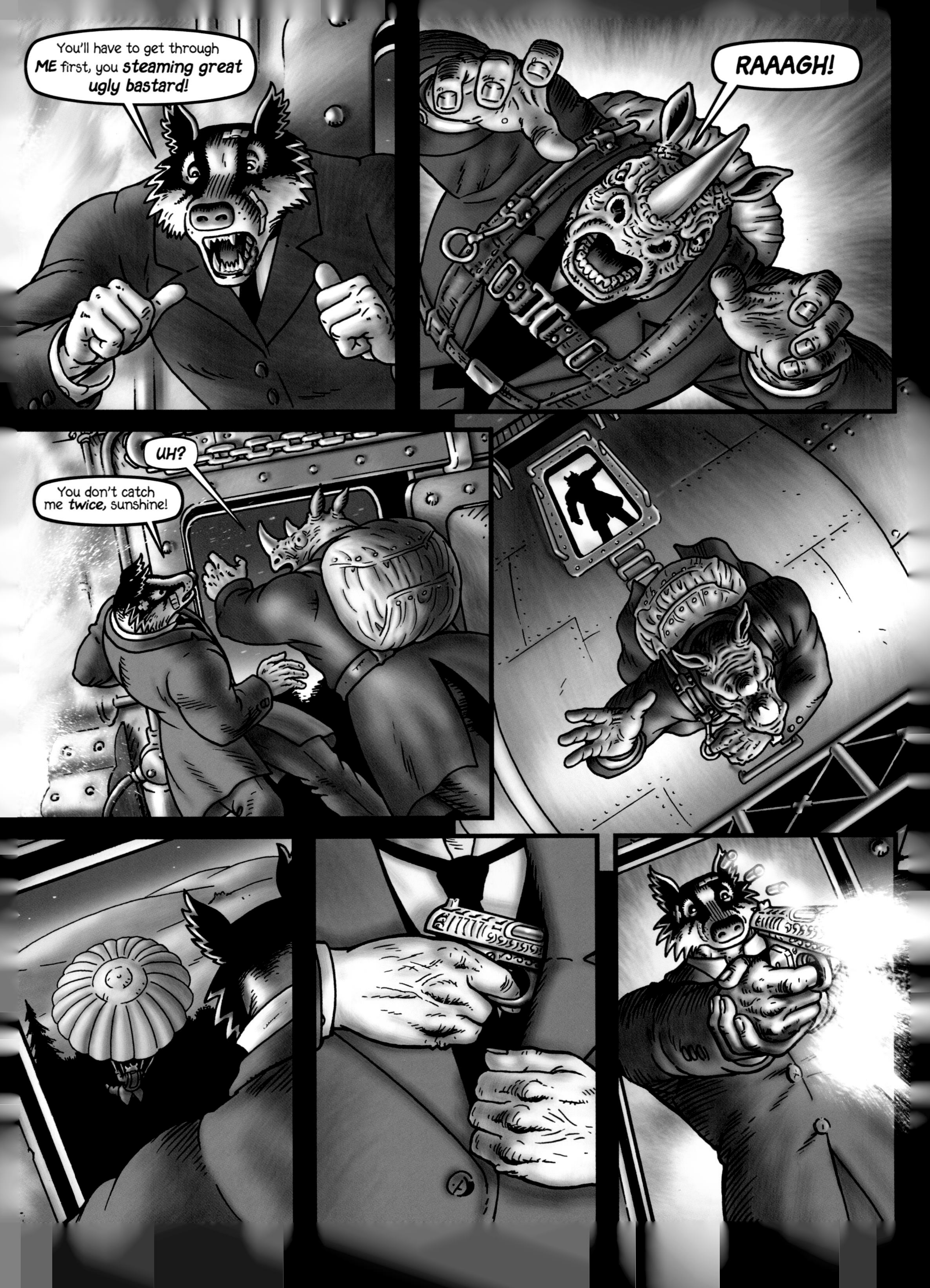
You'll have to get through **ME** first, you **steaming great ugly bastard!**
RAAAGH!
UH?
You don't catch me **twice,** sunshine!

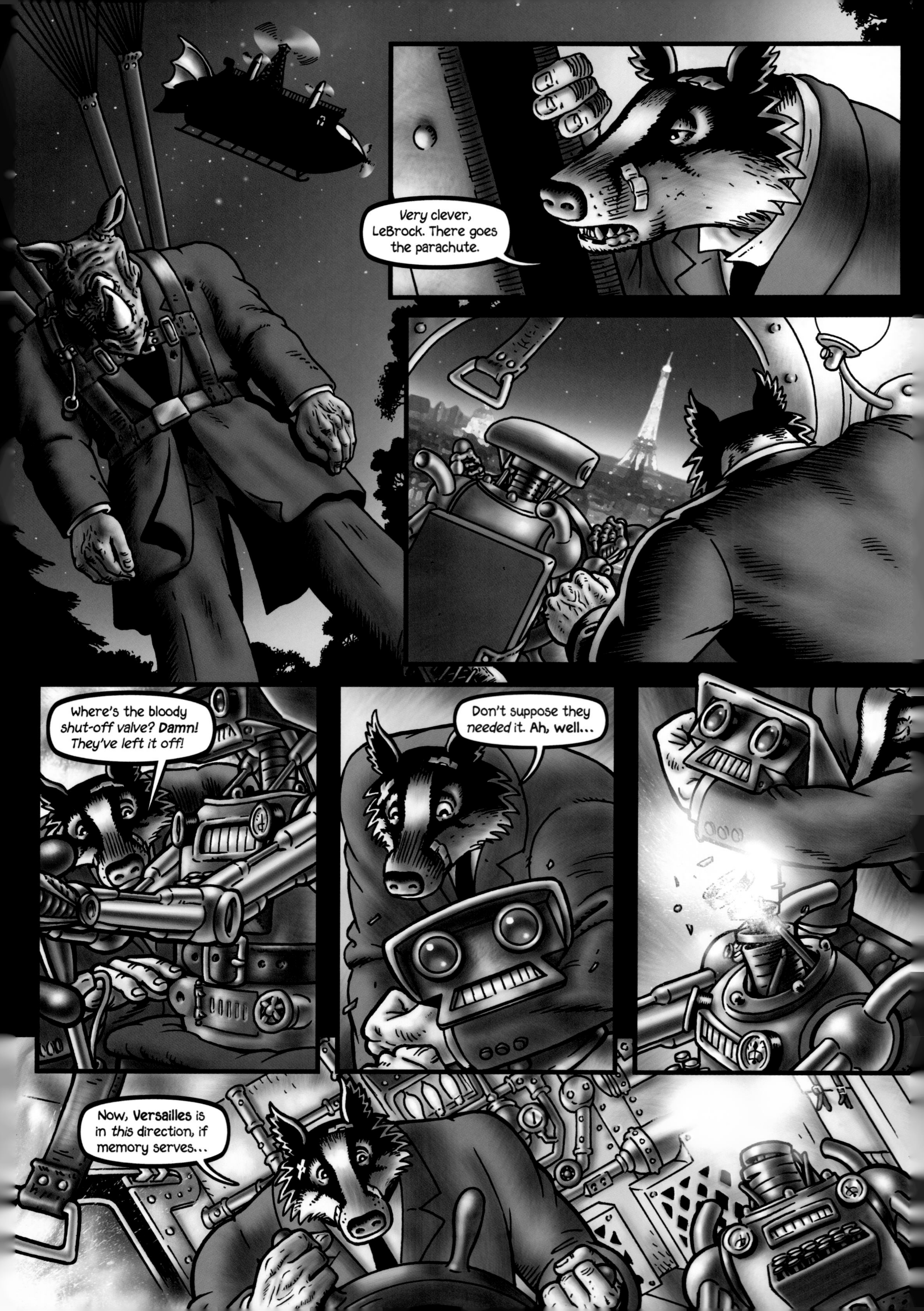
Very clever, LeBrock. There goes the parachute.
Where's the bloody shut-off valve? Damn! They've left it off!
Don't suppose they needed it. Ah, well...
Now, Versailles is in this direction, if memory serves...

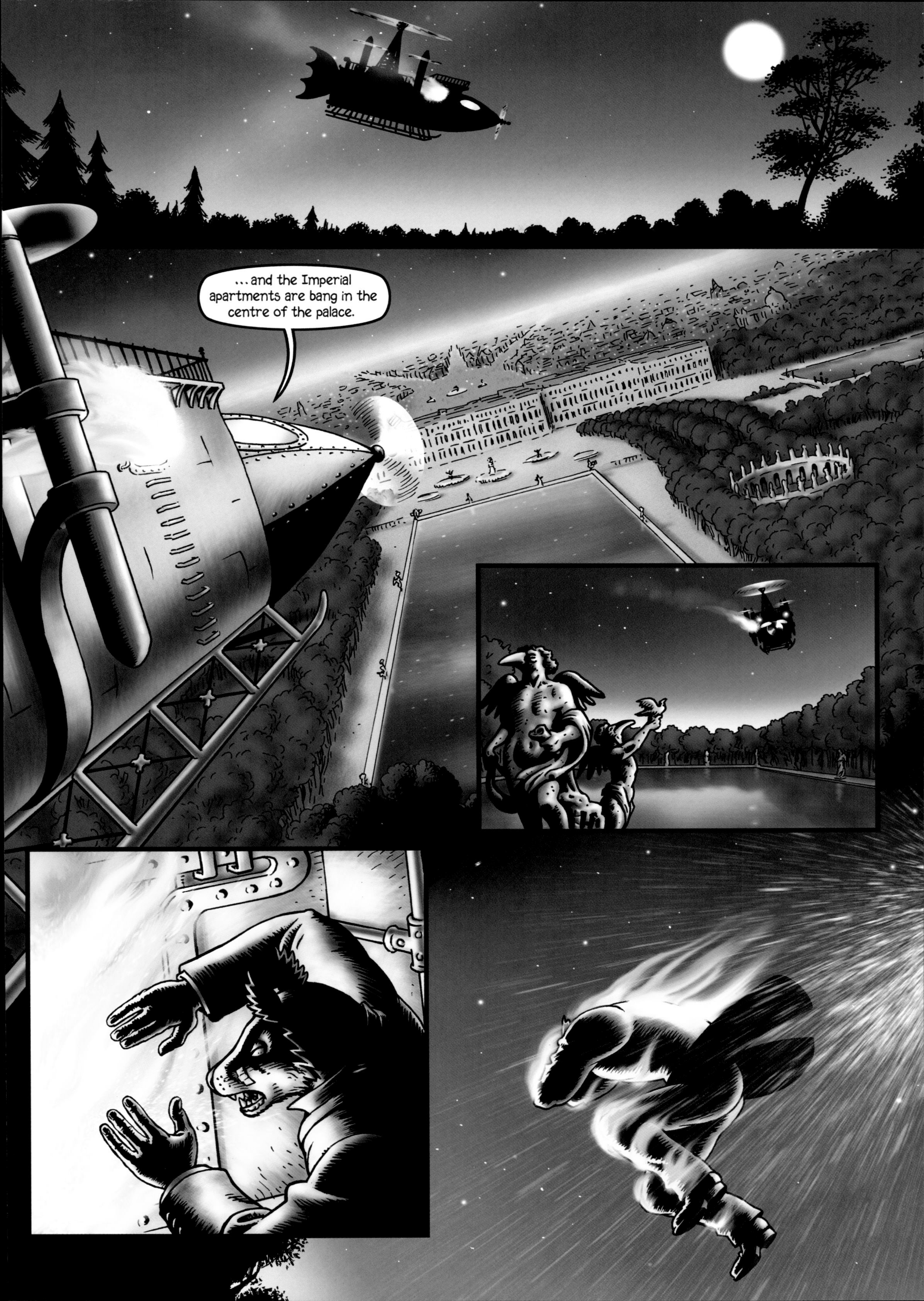
...and the Imperial apartments are bang in the centre of the palace.

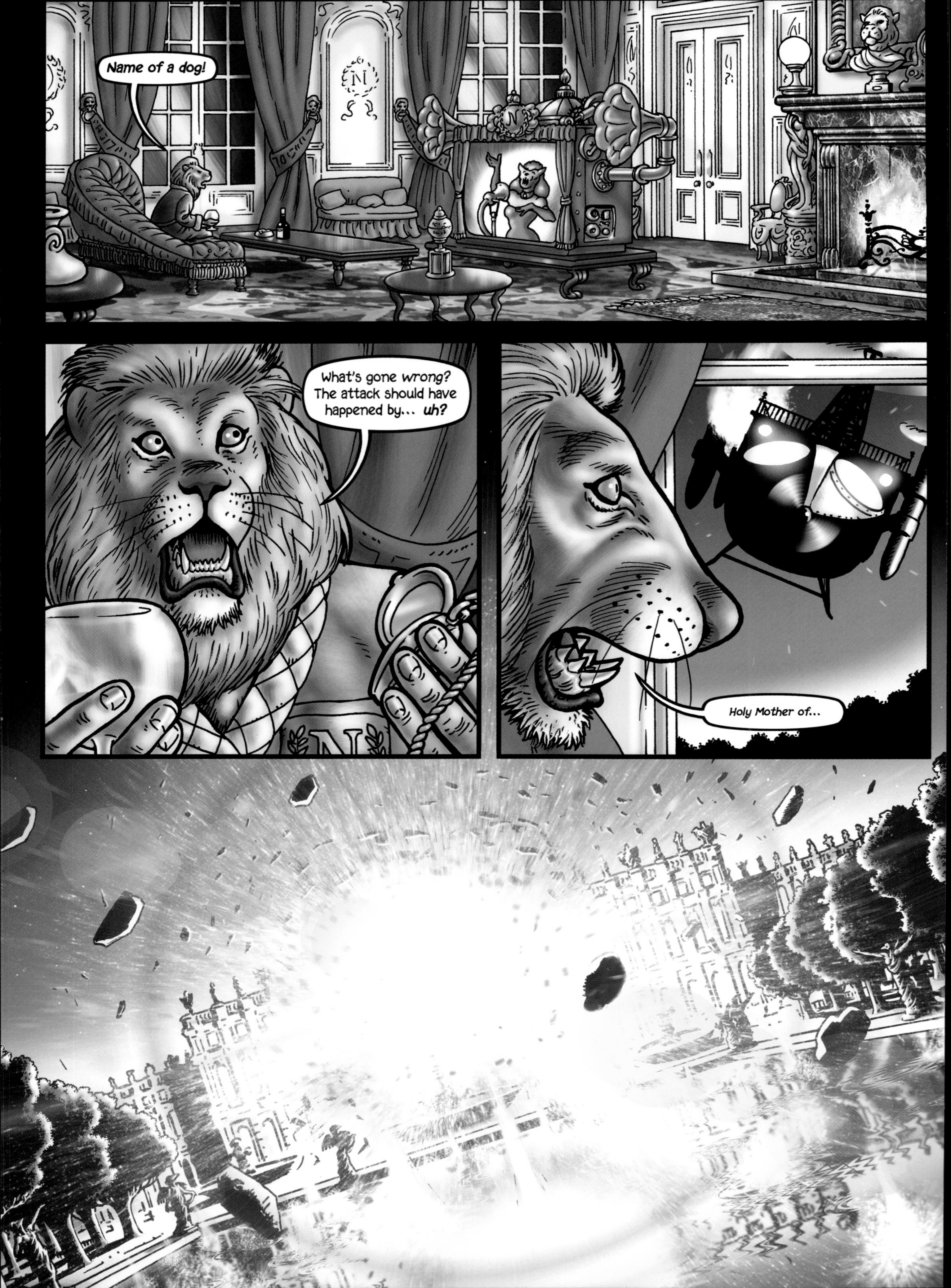
Name of a dog!
What's gone wrong? The attack should have happened by... uh?
Holy Mother of...

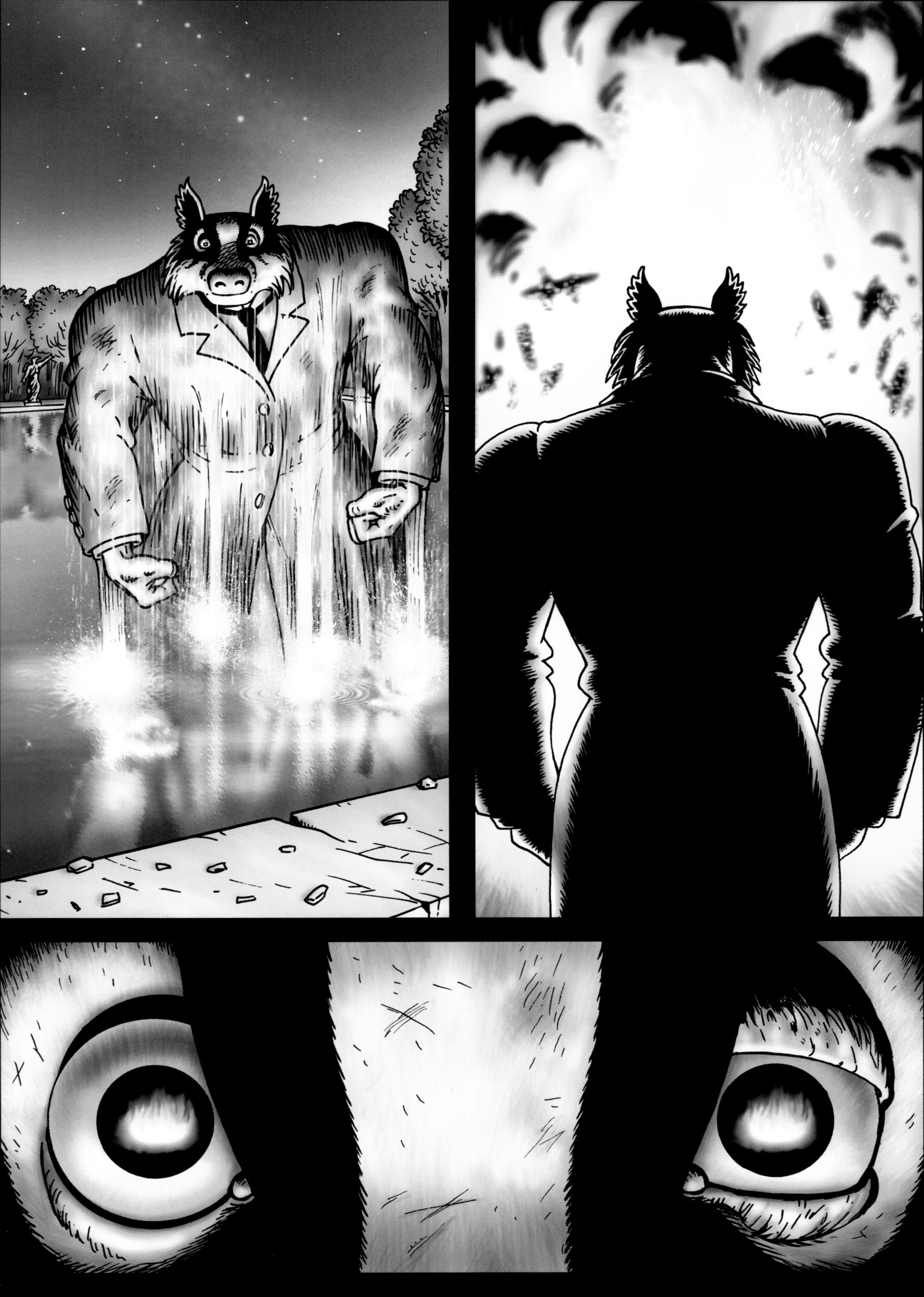

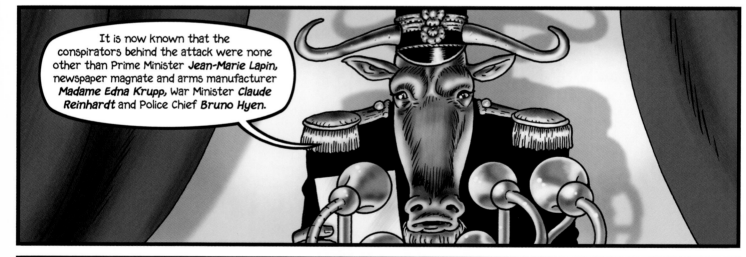

The guards and three of the conspirators were all killed in an exchange of gunfire with one or more unidentified assailants.

Reinhardt, thought to be the pilot of the skyship, was also found dead just outside Paris, shot by person or persons unknown.

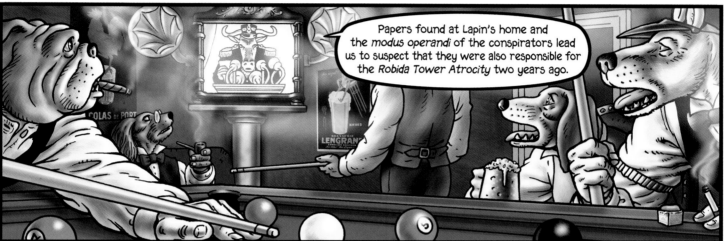

Papers found at Lapin's home and the *modus operandi* of the conspirators lead us to suspect that they were also responsible for the *Robida Tower Atrocity* two years ago.

Well, *there* you have it! *Incredible!*

Police are anxious to interview a *large* animal, thought to be a *bear*, glimpsed leaving the grounds of the Palace after the attack.

Towser Dupont, CNN newshound, signing off.

And so... what *now?*

Will there be a *revolution* after this removal of the head of state and his chief ministers, as many pundits predict?

In some areas there is already open celebration in the streets. Time alone shall tell.

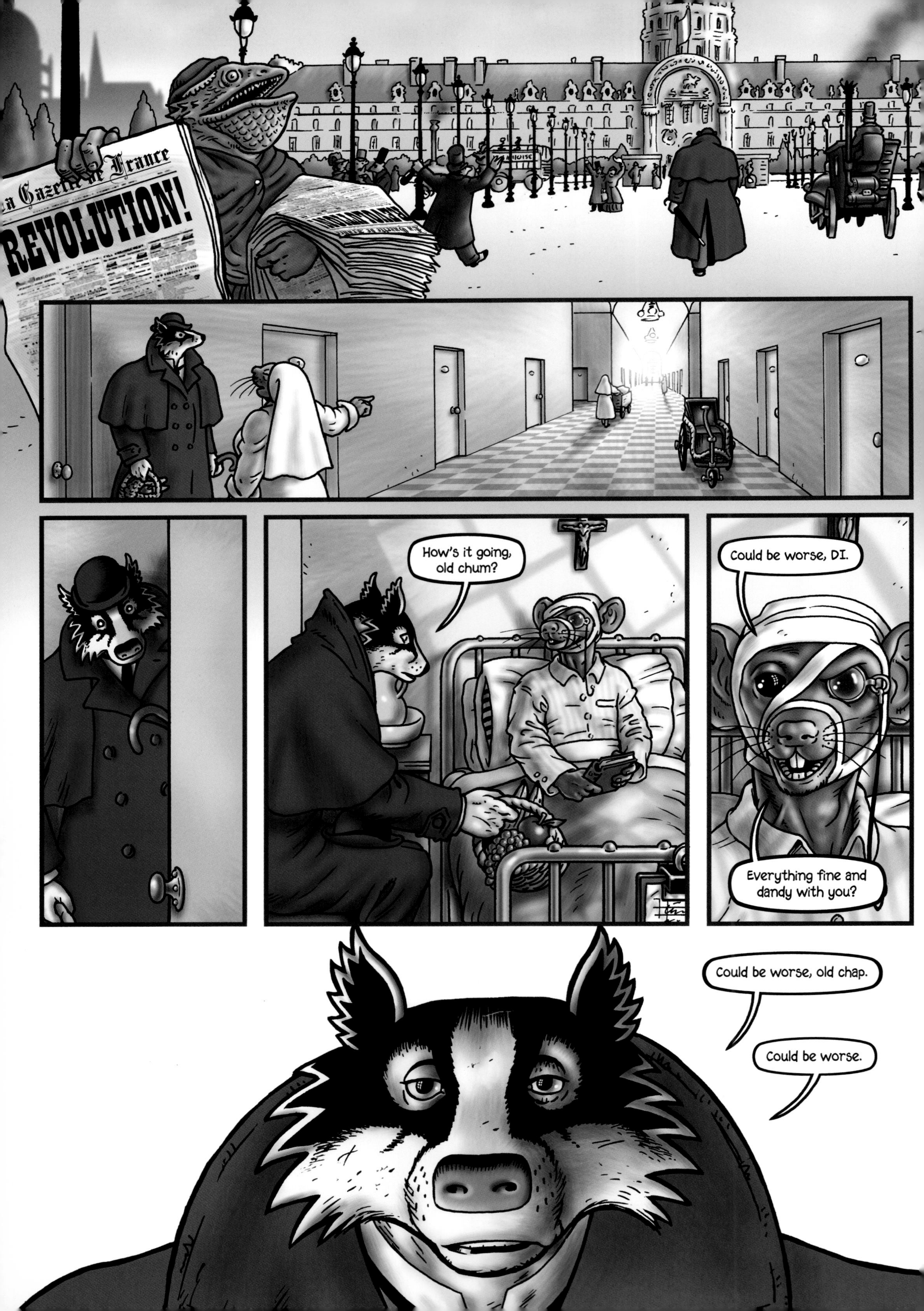
La Gazette de France
REVOLUTION!
How's it going, old chum?
Could be worse, DI.
Everything fine and dandy with you?
Could be worse, old chap.
Could be worse.

Grandville

Fin

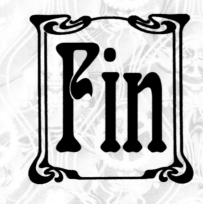

Published by Jonathan Cape 2009

2 4 6 8 10 9 7 5 3 1

Copyright © Bryan Talbot 2009

Bryan Talbot has asserted his right under the Copyright, Designs
and Patents Act 1988 to be identified as the author of this work

This book is sold subject to the condition that it shall not,
by way of trade or otherwise, be lent, resold, hired out,
or otherwise circulated without the publisher's prior
consent in any form of binding or cover other than that
in which it is published and without a similar condition,
including this condition, being imposed
on the subsequent purchaser.

First published in Great Britain in 2009 by
Jonathan Cape
Random House, 20 Vauxhall Bridge Road,
London SW1V 2SA

www.rbooks.co.uk

Addresses for companies within The Random House Group Limited
can be found at: www.randomhouse.co.uk/offices.htm

The Random House Group Limited Reg. No. 954009

A CIP catalogue record for this book is available from the British Library

ISBN 9780224084888

The Random House Group Limited supports The Forest Stewardship
Council (FSC), the leading international forest certification organisation.
All our titles that are printed on Greenpeace approved FSC certified paper
carry the FSC logo. Our paper procurement policy can be found at
www.rbooks.co.uk/environment

Printed and bound in China by C&C Offset Printing Co., Ltd

Other books by Bryan Talbot

Brainstorm!
The Adventures of Luther Arkwright
Heart of Empire
The Tale of One Bad Rat
Alice in Sunderland
The Art of Bryan Talbot
The Naked Artist (Prose)

Metronome

(Writing as Veronique Tanaka)

Cherubs!

(With Mark Stafford)

Nemesis the Warlock Vols 1 & 2

(With Pat Mills)

Sandman: Fables and Reflections

(With Neil Gaiman, Stan Woch & Mark Buckingham)

The Dead Boy Detectives and
the Secret of Immortality

(With Ed Brubaker & Steve Leialoha)

www.bryan-talbot.com